DK EYEWITNESS TOP 10 TRAVEL GUIDES

VANCOUVER

& VICTORIA

CONSTANCE BRISSENDEN

D1439975

Left **False Creek, Vancouver** Right **Storefront, Robson Street**

LONDON, NEW YORK,
MELBOURNE, MUNICH AND DELHI
www.dk.com

Produced by
International Book Productions Inc., Toronto

Reproduced by Colourscan, Singapore
Printed and bound in Italy by Graphicom

First published in Great Britain in 2006
by Dorling Kindersley Limited
80 Strand, London WC2R 0RL
A Penguin Company

Contents

Vancouver & Victoria's Top 10

Cover: Front - **DK Images** Gunter Marx bl; **Getty Images**: Brian Stablyk main;
Joseph S. King clb; Spine - **DK Images** Peter Wilson; Back - **DK
Images** Gunter Marx tr; Peter Wilson tc; **www.guntermarx-stockphotos.com** tl

Key to abbreviations
Adm *admission charge payable*

Left **BC Parliament Buildings at night** Right **Skyride, Grouse Mountain**

Contents

Left **Totem Poles, Stanley Park** Right **Skier, Whistler Mountain**

 Following pages Aerial view of downtown Vancouver with Canada Place in the foreground

3

VANCOUVER AND VICTORIA'S TOP 10

VANCOUVER & VICTORIA'S TOP 10

🔟 Vancouver & Victoria Highlights

Fringed by the Pacific Ocean's sandy beaches, with a backdrop of the Coast Mountain range, Vancouver is among the most beautifully located metropolises on earth. Also feted as the world's most livable city, this West Coast gem has a lively cultural scene and superb restaurants and hotels. On Vancouver Island, a short ferry ride away, Victoria offers visitors a pleasantly peaceful sojourn. The city is an excellent starting-off point from which to explore the many natural wonders of the island.

1 Stanley Park

Created in 1886, Stanley Park is North America's third-largest urban park. It juts into Burrard Inlet, offering an enticing combination of forest, ocean, and beaches, and an encircling seawall pedestrian loop *(see pp8–11)*.

2 Canada Place

Built for Expo '86, Canada Place is now an outstanding convention and hotel complex overlooking Vancouver Harbour. Cruise ships dock alongside an inviting promenade *(see pp12–13)*.

3 Capilano Suspension Bridge

Teetering over a wooden bridge high above the Capilano River is perhaps the most thrilling experience at this sight; walking along a boardwalk up into the treetops a close second. Learn about local history, forest ecology, and First Nations culture as you enjoy the beautiful surroundings *(see pp14–15)*.

4 Storyeum

In an underground bunker beneath Victorian-era Gastown, multi-media exhibits take visitors on a fascinating tour of BC history. Live actors perform their historic roles with gusto *(see pp16–17)*.

5 Vancouver Art Gallery

From the swirling raincoast forests of famed BC artist Emily Carr to radical conceptual installations, the gallery features the best of West Coast and international art *(see pp18–19)*.

Map labels:
Devonian Harbour Park
Stanley Park
WEST GEORGIA
ROBSON
DENMAN STREET
West End
Alexandra Park
DAVIE STREET
BEACH AVENUE
English Bay
PACIFIC STREET
Vanier Park
BURRARD STREET
Ne
GRANVILLE STREET
6 Granville Island
Sutcliffe Park

6 Granville Island
The popular island on False Creek is a bustling mix of shops, galleries, restaurants, and theaters – fun both to visit and explore *(see pp20–21)*.

7 Science World
Science comes alive inside the dome-shaped Science World. Hands-on exhibits capture the imaginations of all ages, with fresh approaches to science in all its dimensions *(see pp22–3)*.

8 Royal British Columbia Museum
A wonderful museum, confidently portraying BC's history and natural assets in creative galleries *(see pp24–5)*.

9 Long Beach Area
Spectacular scenery dominates the Long Beach area on Vancouver Island's West Coast. Wild Pacific shores and rare old-growth forests make the region the perfect destination to experience the essence of rugged BC *(see pp26–7)*.

10 Whistler
Ideal for a day-trip or a longer visit, Whistler is an upscale resort a scenic three-hour drive north from Vancouver. Two mountains tower over alpine-style resort villages. Skiers abound here but countless other year-round activities ensure Whistler has something for everyone *(see pp28–31)*.

Stanley Park

A local favorite since the Victorian era, spectacular Stanley Park is a mere 10-minute bus ride from downtown. Forest walks, beachside strolls, and a vibrant rose garden are among its natural attractions. Amusing activities include a popular children's waterpark and petting zoo, tennis courts, and a pitch-and-putt course. Located in the park, the Vancouver Aquarium Marine Science Centre (see pp10–11) is world-renowned for its realistic walk-through exhibits based on scientific research projects.

Inukshuk, *English Bay*

🍴 Four fine-dining restaurants and many refreshment kiosks offer plenty of food options. The Teahouse at Ferguson Point serves afternoon tea. UpStream Café in the aquarium has coffees and sandwiches.

🕐 Traffic in the park is one way, counterclockwise. Pay parking is strictly enforced.

Bicycle & in-line skate rentals: 604 688 2453

- Map G1
- 604 257 8400
- www.parks.vancouver.bc.ca
- Open 24 hrs daily (not all sights)
- Adm to some activities
- Vancouver Aquarium: 845 Avison Way, 604 659 3474, www.vanaqua.org; Open late Jun–Aug: 9:30am–7pm; Sep–mid-Jun: 10am–5:30pm; Adm: Adult $17.50; Seniors, youths & students $12.95; Children $9.95 (under 4s free)

Top 10 Features

1. English Bay
2. Siwash Rock
3. Beaver Lake
4. Seawall
5. Lost Lagoon
6. Brockton Point
7. Totem Park
8. Vancouver Aquarium
9. Prospect Point
10. Rose Garden

English Bay
The sandy beaches draw crowds to enjoy strolls and the view. The heated saltwater pool at Second Beach offers a warmer alternative to a swim in the bay. Kids delight in the play area nearby. Sunbathers relax at Third Beach against driftwood logs.

Siwash Rock
According to Squamish legend, this ancient lava rock deposit *(above)* jutting up from the water was once an Indian warrior, turned to stone.

Beaver Lake
Hiking trails to Beaver Lake through a raincoast forest follow old logging roads. Frogs, raccoons, rabbits, and even coyote may be spotted at the natural-state lake fringed by cattails and water lilies.

Seawall
Pedestrians, cyclists, and in-line skaters happily share the 6-mi (10-km) paved path ringing the park *(center)*, with its unimpeded views of English Bay and Burrard Inlet. Look for unusual features, such as the sculpture *Girl in a Wetsuit* on an offshore rock.

Lost Lagoon
This willow-fringed lagoon is an inner city wildlife sanctuary, protecting a bevy of wood ducks, blue herons, and white swans. At night, the central fountain is colorfully lit up.

A delightful nighttime ride on the miniature railway takes you through a forest sparkling with lights

Brockton Point

6 The point offers a terrific view of Burrard Inlet. In 1915, a lighthouse *(above)* was built to guide vessels into the harbor. Sailors set their chronometers by the Nine-O'Clock Gun at nearby Hallelujah Point. Its boom has been heard nightly since 1894.

Totem Park

7 Eight carved West Coast poles tell their own stories. Images by First Nations artists denote various family crests and creatures. Haida artist Bill Reid carved the replica of a pre-1878 Skedans mortuary pole with a rectangular frontal board *(above)*.

Vancouver Aquarium

8 Marine displays capture the drama of the West Coast. Six Beluga whales share the space with 60,000 other inhabitants *(see pp10–11)*.

Prospect Point

9 The view from here, the park's highest point, across the dark blue water of Burrard Inlet to the Coast Mountains is one of the best in the city.

Rose Garden

10 A formal rose garden *(below)* blossoms year-round. From April to September, a variety of perennial plantings ensure vibrant color.

Chief Joe Capilano

Few knew Stanley Park like Squamish chief Joe Capilano. Born in 1840, Capilano often visited the park, home to some members of his nation. In 1906, he traveled to England to present a petition on Indian rights to King Edward VII. He shared local stories with Mohawk writer Pauline Johnson, who published them in *Legends of Vancouver* in 1911, a year after Capilano died.

Operating from mid-June to mid-September, the free Stanley Park Shuttle makes 14 stops in Stanley Park; call 604 257 8400

Vancouver & Victoria's Top 10

Left **Clownfish Cove** Right **Shark Penthouse in the Tropic Zone Gallery**

Vancouver Aquarium

1 Wild Coast
Walkways lead past marine creatures from the wild BC West Coast. The animals include frolicking sea otters – one of them rescued from the Exxon Valdez Alaska oil spill in 1989 – playful dolphins, harbor seals, and the Steller sea lions that are members of a shrinking worldwide population. There are live touchpools and demonstrations by naturalists, shows featuring divers swimming with the animals, and training sessions with dolphins and sea lions.

2 Arctic Canada Habitat
Beluga whales are the main draw here. Visitors admire them from both inside and outside locations. Indoors, on the lower level, two wide floor-to-ceiling windows allow underwater viewing. Interactive exhibits provide information about the beluga's native arctic environment.

Sea lion, Wild Coast exhibit

3 Pacific Canada Exhibit
This two-story gallery highlights marine life from the Strait of Georgia and brings visitors face to face with an underwater habitat filled with a vast web of plant and animal life. Divers mingle with thousands of schooling herring, salmon, crabs, kelp, sea stars, and other Pacific marine life. Sturgeon, wolf-eels, and anemones also inhabit this exciting exhibit.

4 Amazon Rainforest
Two caimans, members of the crocodilian group, co-exist in a hot, humid jungle setting with a pair of sloths and Scarlet ibises. Experience a tropical rainstorm every hour in this exotic space.

5 Clownfish Cove
This interactive play zone, designed to appeal to children eight years of age and younger, features animals such as seahorses, horseshoe crabs, toads, and, of course, clownfish. A make-believe marine mammal rescue hospital allows kids to nurse a toy sick or injured seal pup. Puzzles, puppets, dress-up costumes, and crafts are on hand to amuse the little ones.

6 Tropic Zone Gallery
A realistic imitation of a tropical reef in the Indo Pacific highlights this region's rainbow-hued fish, such as blue-green chromis, orange shoulder tang, the redtooth triggerfish, and black-tipped reef sharks.

7 Treasures of the British Columbia Coast
Local waters are the focus of this interesting exhibit. Wolf eels and giant Pacific octopus can be spied lurking in the depths. Stare with fascination as the moon jellyfish dance beneath reflective lights.

The Vancouver Aquarium was one of the first ever to introduce trained naturalists as guides

Top 10 Historical Highlights

1. The Stanley Park peninsula is inhabited by the Squamish until 1888
2. Deadman's Island, an Indian burial site, visited by first white settler, 1862
3. City council petitions for a permanent park, 1886
4. Governor General Stanley dedicates the park, 1889
5. Nine O'Clock Gun arrives, 1894 *(see p9)*
6. The Hollow Tree, a red cedar 65 ft (20 m) in circumference, is the park's most-photographed attraction, early 1900s
7. Lumberman's Arch is built as a tribute to BC's logging industry, 1912
8. Construction of the seawall begins, to prevent erosion, 1917
9. Lost Lagoon is created by construction of the causeway, early 1920s
10. Guinness family builds Lions Gate Bridge at the park's north end, 1938

History of Stanley Park

Coal Harbour peninsula was inhabited for thousands of years by Musqueam, Tsleil-Waututh, and Squamish Coast Salish nations in a village known as Khwaykhway (pronounced Whoi-whoi). In 1862, the peninsula became a military reserve to protect the harbor from American invasion, but the village and its dwellers were left undisturbed. Stanley Park was established on the former military reserve after the Great Fire of June 13, 1886, destroyed the entire city. The park opened in 1888, and was dedicated by Lord Stanley the following year. By 1892, there was no sign of life left in Khwaykhway – most of the Natives had died in a smallpox epidemic between 1888 and 1892.

Entering Stanley Park

Stanley Park's original entrance was through an arch and over a bridge spanning Coal Harbour.

8 Beluga Encounters

Join a trainer behind the scenes in the Arctic Canada habitat to learn how these giant mammals communicate and to help the trainers feed them fish. Or book a sleepover with belugas.

beluga whale

9 BC Hydro Salmon Stream

This demonstration stream teaches the public about the importance of conserving salmon habitats. Juvenile Coho salmon, Chum, and pink salmon populate this ideal salmon stream, which meanders over gravel beds in back eddies, shaded by overhanging banks, trees, and log debris.

10 Shark Penthouse

Thrashing black-tipped reef sharks are fed twice weekly in front of visitors in the Shark Penthouse in the Tropic Zone Gallery. A naturalist dives with the sharks daily.

For more information about the aquarium's sleepover programs, call 604 659 3504 or visit www.vanaqua.org/home

TOP 10 Canada Place

Built for Expo '86 as the flagship Canada Pavilion, Canada Place is a Vancouver landmark. The roof's sail-like lines echo Canada's nautical roots. The "prow" extends well into the harbor. Following the highly successful world exhibition, which attracted more than 22 million visitors, Canada Place was transformed into a complex containing a cruise ship terminal, convention center, exhibition areas, and a first-class hotel. The promenade offers a terrific view of the city's harbor.

Patio, Café Pacifica

🍽 For casual dining, try the Café Pacifica in the Pan Pacific Hotel. Or, for a fine-dining experience, try the hotel's Five Sails dinner-only restaurant. A food court across Canada Place Way is open until 9pm.

🅿 Underground pay parking is available at Canada Place. Less expensive parking can be found in the lot at the north foot of Burrard Street.

• 999 Canada Place Way
• Map L2
• 604 775 7200
• www.canadaplace.ca
• Open daily
• CN IMAX Theatre:
604 682 4629

Top 10 Features

1. Vancouver Touristinfo Centre
2. Architecture
3. Cruise Ship Terminal
4. Floatplanes
5. Promenade
6. Promenade into History
7. CN IMAX Theatre
8. Plaza
9. Vancouver Convention and Exhibition Centre
10. Heritage Horns

1 Vancouver Touristinfo Centre

Operated by Tourism Vancouver, this useful bureau located across Canada Place Way at 200 Burrard Street, on the plaza level, offers free brochures and city maps. The knowledgeable, multilingual volunteer staff will help you plan your stay in Vancouver.

2 Architecture

Built for Expo '86 on a former cargo dock, Canada Place's award-winning design is notable for the five Teflon-coated fiberglass sails, resembling a sailing ship in full rigging, suspended over the convention center.

3 Cruise Ship Terminal

The cruise ship terminal at Canada Place welcomes hundreds of thousands of visitors a year. The three-berth terminal is adjacent to the promenade, providing visitors with a close-up view. From the terminal, it's a short walk to the sights and shops of Gastown *(see pp60–5)*.

 From May to September, some 300 cruise ships depart from Canada Place on their way to Alaska; visit www.portvancouver.com

4 Floatplanes
Pontooned planes arriving from Victoria land at Coal Harbour, to the west of Canada Place. Helicopters from Victoria descend on the east side of the complex.

5 Promenade
A lovely promenade takes you along the west and east sides of Canada Place, and around the point, providing a first-rate view of visiting cruise ships, the harbor, and the SeaBus ferry. On a hot day, cooling breezes make the 6,675-ft (2,000-m) walkway a refreshing place to enjoy the scenery.

6 Promenade into History
Gain a wider knowledge of Vancouver history with a free, self-guided tour along the promenade. Intriguing stories are told through archival photographs. Information and details are presented though 44 sculptures, plaques, and historical points of interest.

7 CN IMAX Theatre
Since Expo '86, the CN IMAX Theatre has entertained visitors with exciting giant-screen IMAX movies. The 440-seat theater brings family-oriented films to gigantic life on a five-story screen. IMAX 3D movies, a world first, debuted here.

8 Plaza
Located near the tip of the point, the plaza *(above)*, offers a cooling fountain, benches, and shady trees. It's a serene spot to sit and watch the comings and goings of the harbor's busy traffic.

9 Vancouver Convention and Exhibition Centre
Conventions and exhibitions are housed in grand halls accessed by an indoor promenade that echoes the exterior walkway. Both conventions and consumer tradeshows are held here, including the huge Vancouver Snow Show in October.

10 Heritage Horns
Every day, at noon, the sound of ten cast-aluminum air horns blasts across Vancouver and beyond from the top of Canada Place. Designed and built by Robert Swanson in 1967 as a project to celebrate Canada's 100th birthday, the first four notes of the noon hour blast are from the country's national anthem, *O Canada*.

Expo '86
On May 2, 1986, Prince Charles and Princess Diana opened Expo '86, a hugely successful world's fair that hosted 50 per cent more people than expected. Unfortunately, it closed with a $311-million deficit. However, enduring legacies such as Canada Place (the former China Pavilion) Science World, the SkyTrain, and the urban renewal of the once-derelict area around False Creek, show that Expo '86 ultimately gave back to Vancouver much more than it had cost.

Vancouver & Victoria's Top 10

Every July 1, Canada Day fireworks awe spectators with technically brilliant displays over the harbor at Canada Place

13

Capilano Suspension Bridge

For thrill appeal, few sites rival Capilano Suspension Bridge. At the height that eagles fly, the bridge is a swaying span across the tumbling Capilano River far below. The world's longest and highest suspension footbridge, it crosses into the hushed recesses of a West Coast rainforest. This century-old attraction now includes a walk high above the forest floor, from treetop to treetop, built using new technology. Scotsman George Grant MacKay, who bought the property in 1888, would be amazed. Today's modern bridge is the fourth on the site.

Costumed guides

🍴 Tasty salmon, beef, and chicken burgers are served at the Loggers' Grill. For specialty coffees, pastries, and homemade pizzas, try the Canyon Café. For full-service, enjoy gourmet dining at the Bridge House Restaurant across Capilano Road.

🌀 If heights are a concern when crossing the bridge, focus on the back of the person in front of you. It's well worth making the trip across.

• 3735 Capilano Rd, North Vancouver
• Map B1
• 604 985 7474
• www.capbridge.com
• Open 9am–5pm daily; Summer: 8:30am–dusk; closed Dec 25
• Summer rates: adults $24.95, senior/students $18.50, youth (13–16) $12.95, children (6–12) $6.50; under 6s free

Top 10 Features

1. Suspension Bridge
2. Locals from the Past
3. The Big House
4. Capilano River and Gorge
5. Treetops Adventure
6. Treetops Technology
7. Totem Park
8. Living Forest
9. Story Centre
10. English Country Garden

1 Suspension Bridge

This awe-inspiring bridge is built of sturdy steel cables spanning 450 ft (137 m) and strong enough to support two full Boeing 747s. Those crossing the bridge today cling tightly to the handrails as they experience the same thrills as visitors did in 1889 *(center)*.

2 Locals from the Past

Friendly costumed guides in period attire welcome visitors to the park. Taking on the roles of local historical characters, the guides narrate the sometimes hair-raising stories of the North Shore's early days when timber was king.

3 The Big House

Skilled carvers, beaders, and weavers work in the open-fronted Little Big House, sharing their skills and cultural knowledge with appreciative onlookers. At the center of the cedar-planked Big House is the Next Generation story pole, honoring First Nations artists. From spring to fall, dancers, drummers, and singers perform legends in the plaza area *(above)*.

Legends performed by First Nations entertainers in front of the Big House are traditional to the West Coast

4 Capilano River and Gorge

As you cross the bridge, look down into the Capilano River gorge 230 ft (70 m) below. After reaching the other side, enjoy the views along the edge of the gorge or from the cantilevered deck that serves as a lookout high over the river.

5 Treetops Adventure

This exhilarating exhibit is located in the West Coast rainforest across the suspension bridge. A boardwalk leads you gently upwards over seven suspension bridges attached to eight old-growth Douglas fir trees *(above)*. At the end of your journey, you are 100 ft (30 m) high in the mysterious zone of mid-story treetops.

6 Treetops Technology

To protect the delicate environment, Treetops Adventure uses an innovative compression system to secure observation platforms to the trees. Instead of nails or screws, friction collars are used. Held on by compression, they exert a gentle pressure equivalent to pressing a thumb firmly on a tabletop.

7 Totem Park

At the park's entrance, a gathering of totem poles carved by local Coast Salish First Nations people makes a colorful display *(below)*. Introduced in the 1930s, the beautifully carved poles now number more than 30.

8 Living Forest

In the Living Forest ecology area, clever interactive displays educate about native plants and trees, such as Douglas firs. Panels feature the animals and bugs living in a West Coast rainforest. Naturalists offer guided tours year round on its peaceful forest trails.

9 Story Centre

From miners to loggers to dancehall girls, the center tells the history of the park and of North Vancouver in a walk-through exhibit. Hundreds of photographs bring history to life, while captions put the people and places into perspective. Voices from the Past, an audio component, fills in any blanks.

10 English Country Garden

The picturesque perennial garden harks back to the homeland of many of Vancouver's early settlers. Planted in 1910, the azaleas and rhododendrons dazzle with massive colorful blooms. The century-old shrubs are at their best in May.

A Lasting Legacy

Scotsman George Grant MacKay loved the outdoors. As Vancouver's first park commissioner, he voted in favor of Stanley Park in 1886. Two years later, he bought 6,000 acres (2,428 ha) of old-growth forest along the Capilano River and built a cabin on the edge of the canyon wall. Then, with the help of local Coast Salish, he built a small hemp rope and cedar suspension bridge in 1889. This was the very first bridge.

TOP 10 Storyeum

Storyeum's theatrical experience takes place beneath the historic streets of Gastown. In a fast-moving 65-minutes, multi-media effects combine with costumed actors to create a multi-sensory panorama of BC history. The engrossing tales are based on real characters from travelers' diaries, Aboriginal oral history, and documents of pioneers. Starting with pre-European contact before the 1700s, the shows introduce the province's people and places in lively scenarios combining drama, humor, and action.

Storyeum entrance

🍴 Cafés and restaurants serving everything from deli sandwiches to ethnic specialties abound on Water St.

🕐 The lift departs for the show area on the hour and half hour. Reservations are recommended.

After you return to the surface, there is a short outdoor walk back into the main lobby on Water St.

- 142 Water St
- Map L3
- 604 687 8142
- www.storyeum.com
- Open 10am–5pm (last show) Tue–Fri, 10am–5:30pm (last show) Sat–Mon
- Adm: $21.95 (under 6s free)

Top 10 Highlights

1. Story Gallery
2. Going Underground
3. Ancient Trails
4. The Big House
5. The National Dream
6. Barkerville Gold Seekers
7. New Arrivals
8. Last Stop…Vancouver!
9. BC Spirit
10. Gastown Merchants

②Going Underground

Enter a rusted-out "water tank," one of the world's largest lifts, to begin your journey. As you descend beneath the streets of historic Gastown, a narrator relates the concept behind Storyeum using an aboriginal story about trees.

①Story Gallery

Displayed on the walls of the main Water Street lobby are hundreds of photographs portraying the people of BC from the early days to the present. Sourced and selected from archives located all over the province, this is one of the largest public collections of archival photographs in the province.

③Ancient Trails

Visitors enter a spectacularly re-created rainforest where a Tsleil-Waututh legend comes to life. Man is created from wolf and woman from sediment at the bottom of the sea. Culture and tradition spring from the first couple.

④The Big House

A reproduction of a Coast Salish Big House creates the feel of these buildings. First Nations actors *(left)* portray the descendants of the first couple. A traditional feast honors their union.

Storyeum is a walking journey; sets have a varying number of seats. Each set provides designated seating for those who require it

5 The National Dream

The completion of the coast-to-coast railway signals Canada's coming-of-age *(above)*. Integral to the history of the railway are the fates of the Chinese workers who toiled on its construction. As the story unfolds, industries boom in BC, and BC women obtain the right to vote.

6 Barkerville Gold Seekers

Lively acting conveys the excitement of the Cariboo Gold Rush of 1862 *(below)*. Among the true-to-life cast of characters is "the hanging judge" Matthew Begbie and Miss Florence Wilson, just off a bride ship, who attempts to civilize the predominantly male town residents.

7 New Arrivals

The arrival of Europeans brings dramatic change to the West Coast as depicted on the decks of a re-created trading ship *(center)*. The all-powerful Hudson's Bay Company's chief factor James Douglas arrives on Vancouver Island. The fort is built in 1843 and the trading vessel *Endurance* arrives.

8 Last Stop… Vancouver!

In this final show with live actors, one of the first trains arrives in Gastown in 1887. Men and women return from World War II, reuniting British Columbians. Together, all look ahead to a prosperous future.

9 BC Spirit

During the return to street level in a second, 46-ft- (14 m-) high lift, a 360-degree multi-media presentation dances above the heads of passengers. Stunning images of BC's present-day society and its gorgeous landscapes are featured.

10 Gastown Merchants

Back above ground, you re-enter the Water Street lobby where the Gastown Merchants gift shop *(left)*, selling good quality history-themed items, is located.

The Gold Rush

On April 25, 1858, several hundred men landed in Victoria on a steamer. The tumultuous Cariboo Gold Rush had begun. Soon, 20,000 other gold-seekers, including many Chinese, followed, en route to the mainland and the town of Barkerville, to stake the banks and tributaries of the Fraser River. By 1860, the gold was panned out and the miners, now mainly Chinese, moved further north along the river. By 1865, the rush was over.

The seven original songs played during your Storyeum journey include orchestration by the Vancouver Symphony Orchestra

🔟 Vancouver Art Gallery

The Vancouver Art Gallery is the largest art gallery in Western Canada. Its only permanent exhibit, a homage to the life and works of Emily Carr, BC's pre-eminent artist and writer, is well worth the entry fee. The gallery specializes in impressive national and international exhibitions, with innovative approaches to old masters as well as contemporary visionaries. Founded in 1931, the art gallery includes more than 8,000 works in its collection, including several pieces by renowned local painter Jack Shadbolt. Housed in a NeoClassical heritage building redesigned by acclaimed Vancouver architect Arthur Erickson, the gallery opened in 1983 as an elegant addition to downtown.

Rotunda

The Gallery Café patio is a gem on sunny summer days. You do not need to purchase admission to the gallery to eat at the café.

The Gallery Store sells contemporary art books, posters, paper goods, jewelry, and giftware, including a wide selection of Emily Carr merchandise.

- *750 Hornby St*
- *Map K3*
- *604 662 4700*
- *www.vanartgallery. bc.ca*
- *Open Sat–Wed & hols 10am–5:30pm, Thu & Fri 10am–9pm; closed Dec 25 & Jan 1*
- *Adm: $15 (under 5s free). By donation 5–9pm Thu*

Top 10 Features

1. Court House Building
2. Emily Carr Permanent Exhibit
3. Art on the Rooftop
4. Photoconceptual Collection
5. Southern Façade
6. Exhibitions Program
7. Beck/Groff Collection
8. Architecture
9. First Nations Art
10. Super Sundays

1 Court House Building

Built in 1912 as the Provincial Court House, the building reflects the imposing style of the era's leading Canadian architect, Francis Rattenbury.

2 Emily Carr Permanent Exhibit

The Gallery holds over 200 works by Emily Carr. This renowned West Coast artist studied local Native cultures, capturing their way of life in her paintings. Haida artifacts such as totem poles were a common subject. Stormy West Coast colors as seen, for example, in *Logger's Culls (center)*, dominate her work. Items such as her tiny sketch book are also on display.

3 Art on the Rooftop

Vancouver artist Ken Lum's innovative *Four Boats Stranded: Red and Yellow, Black and White* stands out on the gallery's roof *(above)*. The installations include a scaled-down version of a First Nations longboat.

Tours of the gallery are free with admission and take place hourly

4 Photoconceptual Collection

The gallery is known for its permanent collection of contemporary photo-based art that spans two decades and includes works by the Vancouver School of artists, such as Jeff Wall, Stan Douglas, Ian Wallace, and Ken Lum, as well as international artists Nancy Spero and Cindy Sherman, among others.

PLACED UPON THE HORIZON (CASTING SHADOWS)

5 Southern Façade

Overlooking Robson Street, the original steps into the court house are now a popular meeting spot for locals. On the portico (above) is a cryptic message carved in yellow cedar letters by conceptual artist Lawrence Weiner.

6 Exhibitions Program

Foremost artists, ranging from historic masters to leading-edge contemporary artists, are regularly presented in major thematic exhibitions, solo shows, and intimate, focused showcases.

7 Beck/Gruft Collection

This major collection of historical photographs includes significant images by acclaimed photographers such as Andre Kertesz, Maxime Du Camp, and Walker Evans.

8 Architecture

Architectural icon Arthur Erickson added 41,400 sq ft (3,715 sq m) of exhibit space to the old court house when transforming it into the gallery's permanent home. Erickson retained many of the original features, including the courtroom, with its carved judge's bench.

9 First Nations Art

Paintings, carvings, and sculpture by Pacific Northwest Native artists are part of the gallery's rotating permanent collection, which includes sculptures by late Haida master carver Bill Reid (see p36). Reflecting the modernist style of many Native artists, *Eagles* (below), by Haida artist Robert Davidson, combines principles of abstraction with traditional iconography.

10 Super Sundays

On the third Sunday of each month, families with school-aged children come to learn about art together. Draw, paint, create art projects, and watch or engage in dance performances.

Emily Carr

Emily Carr was born into a wealthy Victoria family in 1871. The eccentric artist, however, chose a bohemian lifestyle, and her powerful artworks were painted on a pauper's budget, often in the old-growth forests of Haida Gwaii (Queen Charlotte Islands). It wasn't until 1937, when Carr was 65 years old, that the Vancouver Art Gallery bought one of her works. Largely overlooked during her lifetime, Carr's works now command some of the highest prices in Canada.

Exhibitions are enhanced with lectures by gallery curators, artists, and art historians; call 604 662 4717 for details

Granville Island

Bustling Granville Island attracts millions of visitors every year, and rightly so. Where heavy industries once belched noxious fumes, street entertainers now amuse passersby with music, comedy, and magic. The Granville Island Public Market offers an enchanting mix of edibles and collectibles. More than 200 shops scattered throughout the Island sell everything from custom-made jewelry to yachts.

Aquabus

🍽 La Baguette et l'Echalote, adjacent to the market, at 1680 Johnston St, is one of the best French patisseries in town.

🕐 Locals know that the doors, and most businesses, inside the public market building are unofficially open by 8am. Arrive early if you want a sneak peek before the market gets busy.

The summer-only WaterPark is free. Find it just off Cartwright Street, behind the Information Centre.

• Map H5
• 604 666 5784
• www. granvilleisland.com
• Public market: open 9am–6pm daily; closed Dec 25 & 26, Jan 1
• Information Centre: open 9am–6pm daily
• Net Loft and Kids Market: open 10am–7pm daily; varying hrs for businesses

Top 10 Features

1. Granville Island Public Market
2. Marina and Maritime Market
3. Kids Market
4. New-Small and Sterling Studio Glass
5. Railspur Alley
6. Granville Island Brewing Co.
7. Emily Carr Institute of Art and Design
8. Net Loft
9. Arts Club Theatre and Lounge
10. Granville Island Museums

2 Marina and Maritime Market

Shops and services at the market include a kayak center *(above)*, seafood merchants, tours, boat rentals, and marine souvenir shops. At the marina, yachts and sailboats are moored beside rustic fishing boats.

3 Kids Market

Clowns and magicians guarantee fun in a fantasyland for children. More than 20 shops sell everything from games and toys to pint-sized clothing.

1 Granville Island Public Market

The centerpiece of the island's shopping experience, the public market is an irresistible emporium of green grocers, butchers, bakers, fishmongers, importers, ethnic foodsellers, craft vendors, sweet stands, florists, and casual eateries *(center)*. It also has a wine shop and a micro-roaster of organic coffee *(see p80)*.

4 New-Small and Sterling Studio Glass

Watch David New-Small and apprentices as they blow molten glass into beautiful vases, ornaments, jewelry and dishes using traditional techniques. One of four furnaces keeps 150 lbs (70 kg) of glass molten at 2,000°F (1,100°C) around the clock. Visit the adjoining gallery to admire or buy handmade glass jewelry, ornaments, bowls, vases, and plates.

 Free parking on the Island is limited to three hours; pay parking at the east end avoids the very real possibility of a parking ticket

5 Railspur Alley

The cozy artisan studio-shops *(above)* in this small laneway are operated by painters, potters, and craftspeople specializing in wood, fabric, leather, glass, and industrial cast-offs.

6 Granville Island Brewing Company

This microbrewery – Canada's first – opened in 1984. Sample the delicious beers made using only natural ingredients at many Vancouver pubs or in the brewery's Taproom after a behind-the-scenes tour, offered daily at noon, 2pm, and 4pm.

7 Emily Carr Institute of Art and Design

Named after famed West Coast artist Emily Carr *(see p19),* this premier art school is a busy hub for Canada's up-and-coming artists. Step inside to visit the Charles H. Scott Gallery *(right),* in one of the Island's original industrial buildings, to see work by contemporary artists. Students of the Institute present their works in the Concourse and Media Galleries.

8 Net Loft

An intimate collection of boutiques sells unusual souvenirs, such as handmade paper, hats, off-beat postcards, beads of all kinds, and local and First Nations crafts.

9 Arts Club Theatre and Lounge

The Arts Club Theatre Company produces contemporary comedies and new works to classics at the Granville Island Stage. The casual Backstage Lounge showcases local bands *(see p43 and p82).*

Granville Island Ferries

The small vessels of the Aquabus and False Creek Ferries fleets provide year-round service around False Creek, with frequent sailings to and from downtown. They are a fun way to travel to Granville Island. Other routes include stops at Science World, Yaletown, and Vanier Park. Mini sunset cruises are also available.

10 Granville Island Museums

See three museums in one. The Model Trains Museum has the largest collection of model and toy trains on exhibit. The Model Ships Museum features large-scale models of warships, sailing vessels, and coastal workboats *(right).* A superb exhibit of fishing history and equipment is at the Sport Fishing Museum *(see p77).*

The False Creek Ferries (604 684 7781) and Aquabus (604 689 5858) vessels depart from the west side of the public market

⁙10 Science World

Fascinating insights into all aspects of the universe are featured at the award-winning Science World. Explorations begin with the smallest insect and progress to the farthest corners of the galaxy. A legacy of Expo '86, the building opened as a science center in 1989 after passionate community efforts. Five galleries feature hundreds of delightfully interactive, hands-on displays and exhibits, while intriguing traveling exhibits show regularly. In 2005, the telecommunications giant TELUS donated $9 million to develop exhibits and programs to ensure that Science World is always fresh and up-to-date.

Illusions Gallery

Top 10 Highlights

1. Geodesic Dome
2. Alcan OMNIMAX Theatre
3. Illusions Gallery
4. Kidspace Gallery
5. Centre Stage
6. Our World Gallery
7. Feature Gallery
8. Eureka! Gallery
9. Science Theatre
10. BodyWorks Gallery

🚇 White Spot, a popular BC chain known for its burgers slathered with Triple O (triple oozy) sauce, is on the Science World site. A concession on Level 2 offers juices, popcorn, and ice cream bars.

🅿️ Paid parking in the small lot is at a premium. It's best to take the SkyTrain to Main Street Station, then walk the short block to Science World.

• 1455 Quebec St
• Map M5
• 604 443 7440
• www.science world.bc.ca
• Open summer: 10am–6pm daily; winter: 10am–5pm Mon–Fri, 10am–6pm Sat–Sun, holidays; closed Jan 1 & Dec 25
• Adm: adults $13.75, seniors/students/youth $9.50; under 4s free Additional fee for Alcan OMNIMAX Theatre

1 Geodesic Dome
Science World's 155-ft- (47-m-) tall geodesic dome *(center)* is affectionately dubbed "the golf ball" by locals. The design is based on the prototype structure made famous by US inventor and architect R. Buckminster Fuller. Mirrorlike exterior panels, 766 in all, reflect the sunlight, while 391 exterior lights sparkle at night.

2 Alcan OMNIMAX Theatre
The five-story screen – the largest in the world – envelops viewers with thrilling films such as Academy Award-nominated *The Living Sea*. The 400-seat theater, located in the geodesic dome, projects images nine times larger than a conventional movie house onto a screen 88 ft (27 m) in diameter. Sound pours out of 28 digital speakers.

3 Illusions Gallery
Everything is not the way it seems in this wonderful world of optical illusions. Straight lines appear to bend, still images begin to move. Puzzle tables pit wits against mind-twisters for all ages.

4 Kidspace Gallery
Kids ages two to six get to burn off excess energy climbing, sliding, running, and jumping on the exhibits *(below)*. Water play, with boats supplied, is a favorite.

 A four-hour visit is the average at Science World

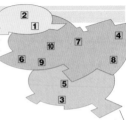

Entrance

5 Centre Stage
Scientific principles and phenomena are explored in five daily shows. Presenters mix balloons and electricity, bubbles and fire to dazzle and captivate as well as teach. Volunteer kids are invited on stage.

Key to Floorplan

▓	Level 1
▓	Level 2
▓	Level 3

9 Science Theatre
Everything from cartoons for toddlers to films about how IMAX movies are made will entrance you in this first-come, first-seated theater. High-definition films reveal the smallest details in feature films and selected shorts. Some live presentations.

10 BodyWorks Gallery
BodyWorks encourages a positive curiosity about the human body. Questions about how human beings hear and smell are answered in this fun-filled interactive space. Strength and dexterity are tested by activities such as bike pedaling and simulated skiing.

6 Our World Gallery
As you check out what has been left in the garbage dump or walk into a giant cheese burger, Our World reveals how the choices we make about waste disposal, food production, and transportation affect our home communities.

7 Feature Gallery
The best in traveling exhibits are showcased in the Feature Gallery. A large plasma TV is a focal point in this gallery, showing breaking news in the world of science almost as it happens. The changing exhibits are certain to be exciting and interactive experiences for all ages.

8 Eureka! Gallery
Eureka! Gallery *(above)* explores universal themes such as water, air, motion, and invention. Children and adults alike are invited to make their own discoveries in a lifelike science laboratory environment. Use the infrared camera to discover the hot spots on your body.

Museum Guide

Science World's first floor is home to Puzzles, Illusions, and Centre Stage. On the second floor are the Eureka!, Kidspace, Our World, Feature, and Search galleries, and Contraption Corner. Alcan OMNIMAX Theatre, on the third floor, is accessible with a Science World ticket or independently by way of a new entrance to the building.

Royal British Columbia Museum

Founded in Victoria in 1886, this impressive museum focuses on BC's cultures, history, geography, flora, and fauna. The museum is regarded as one of the best in Canada for the striking way it presents its exhibits. Some 26,000 sq ft (2,415 sq m) of exhibition space houses more than seven million items. Dramatic walk-through scenarios bring history to life in four galleries, each featuring original and often rarely seen artifacts. An extensive collection of First Nations art and traditional objects, one of the largest and most impressive in the world, has been amassed.

Helmcken House

🏛 Opposite the coat-check, Jazzman's Café specializes in fine coffees, lattes, and pastries. Or try a light-lunch salad or sandwich.

🚗 Pay parking is located behind the museum on Superior Street, at $2 an hour.

Pick up a free map of the museum at the entrance.

- 675 Belleville St, Victoria
- Map P4
- 250 356 7226
- www.royalbc museum.bc.ca
- Open 9am–5pm daily; closed Jan 1 & Dec 25
- Adm: adults $12.50, senior/youth/student $8.70; under 6s free

Top 10 Features

1 Carving Studio
2 Living Land, Living Sea
3 Natural History Gallery
4 First Peoples Gallery
5 Modern History Gallery
6 Helmcken House
7 Carillon Tower
8 Mungo Martin House
9 National Geographic IMAX Theatre
10 Thunderbird Park

1 Carving Studio
Serene Thunderbird Park, on the museum grounds, is home to a beautiful longhouse and a carving studio *(center)*. Many foremost First Nations carvers have worked here, including Chief Mungo Martin, Doug Cranmer, and Bill Reid.

2 Living Land, Living Sea
Climate change is the focus here, with one-of-a-kind artifacts and specimens, and a re-created prehistoric woolly mammoth *(left)*. Ancient is an understatement for the 85.5-million-year-old Cycad fossil. The dramatic 3D map of BC is the first to be generated solely from satellite images.

3 Natural History Gallery
Realistic dioramas explore a range of environments, from ocean to boreal forest, including the giant old-growth forest that once covered coastal BC. One of the best of a range of animals depicted in re-created habitats is a grizzly bear, BC's largest land predator.

First Nations carvers in the carving studio enjoy sharing their knowledge with visitors during the summer season

First Peoples Gallery

4 Historic photos, video, audio, and Native artifacts are combined for a spellbinding experience *(above)*. Superb ceremonial masks and an unforgettable cedar Big House.

Key to Plan

- Ground floor
- Second floor
- Third floor

Modern History Gallery

5 In the atmospheric 20th-Century Hall, it's easy to step back into the Victoria of the 1900s *(right)*. Re-created buildings include the Grand Hotel, with its authentic wooden sidewalk, a salmon cannery, a dressmaker's studio, and a Chinese herbalist's shop, all displaying authentic period objects. Soft lighting sets the mood.

Mungo Martin House

8 Also called Wawadit'la, this replica of a 19th-century longhouse was entrusted to the museum in 1952 by the family of Kwakwa̲ka'wakw Chief Mungo Martin. A dynamic green sea monster in the form of a spiny sculpin (small fish) is painted on the façade. The longhouse is closed to the public as it is reserved for traditional First Nations ceremonies.

Thunderbird Park

10 Over a dozen poles preside over this park. The carved mythical figures tell stories of traditional Coast Salish cultures. Included are Gitx̲san memorial poles, Nuxalk grave figures, Haida mortuary poles, a Cumshewa pole, and Kwakwa̲ka'wakw heraldic poles.

Helmcken House

The oldest house in [ ] still on its original site [wa]s built by Dr. John [Se]bastian Helmcken in [18]52. The three-room [lo]g structure is made of [Do]uglas fir trees. Period [fur]nishings are a remind[er] of the Victorian era.

Carillon Tower

The Netherlands Caril[lon] Tower was gifted to [the] museum in 1967 from [the] residents of Dutch [de]scent. It has a total [of] 62 bells. Free recitals [are] held at 3pm on [Su]ndays.

National Geographic IMAX Theatre

9 Subjects as diverse as whales and outer space are explored in the rotating series of documentary films on the theater's six-story screen.

Museum Guide

The main exhibits are located on the second and third floors of the museum. Natural History Gallery and Living Land, Living Sea are on the second floor, the First Peoples and Modern History galleries on the third. More exhibits are located outside.

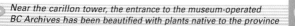

Near the carillon tower, the entrance to the museum-operated BC Archives has been beautified with plants native to the province

⑩ Around Long Beach

The wild west coast of Vancouver Island's Long Beach area offers pristine wilderness, old-growth rainforest, endless beaches, and mystical vistas. Bald eagles appear in large numbers in Clayoquot Sound, a UNESCO Biosphere reserve, while the Pacific Ocean teems with Dall's porpoises, sea lions, and seals. Surfing, fishing, kayaking, and storm watching are superb.

Boogie boarders, Long Beach

🍴 Try local oysters, Dungeness crab, halibut, and wild salmon when in the Long Beach area. Cozy Schooner Restaurant in Tofino (331 Campbell St, 250 725 4644) is decorated with photos of schooners in their glory. In Ucluelet, the Boat Basin Restaurant (1971 Harbour Dr, 250 726 4644), overlooks a scenic marina.

⏰ Book early for the weeklong Pacific Rim Whale Festival (250 726 7798) in late March.

• Map A4
• Tourist information: www.my-tofino.com and www.uclueletbc.com

Top 10 Sights

1. Wickaninnish Interpretive Centre
2. Tofino
3. Long Beach
4. Clayoquot Sound
5. Vargas Island
6. Eagle Aerie Gallery
7. Pacific Rim National Park Reserve of Canada
8. Ucluelet
9. Wild Pacific Trail
10. West Coast Trail

② Tofino

Tofino was named by Spanish explorer Juan Francisco de la Bodega y Quadra after one of his teachers, a hydrographer. Located at the entrance to Clayoquot Sound, this pretty coastal town, with 1,600 residents, provides easy access to white-sand beaches and is a magnet for outdoor adventurers and winter storm watchers. At the government docks *(center)*, seafood is sold right off the boats.

① Wickaninnish Interpretive Centre

The cedar-built center makes a great first stop for Long Beach visitors. Indoor displays introduce natural history as well as historic cultural objects of the local Nuu-Chah-Nulth people. Step out on the viewing platform to spot whales passing along the coast. Not to be missed are the center's beach tours.

③ Long Beach

Rolling waves wash the white sand shores of this seemingly endless wind-swept beach, 15.5 mi (25 km) in length *(below)*. The crashing Pacific Ocean rollers offer unbeatable year-round surfing. Giant Sitka spruce and cedars growing in moss-draped temperate rainforests border the beach.

➡ *Allow about six hours for the slow but scenic 200-mile (320-km) drive from Victoria to Tofino along Highways 1 and 4*

Clayoquot Sound

Pronounced "clack-wot," Clayoquot boasts trees ~5 ft (90 m) tall and 1,700 years old. They share the territory with black bears, elk *(above)*, wolves, and an elusive endangered bird, the marbled murrelet. The coastline mingles bays, beaches, channels, intertidal lagoons, and mudflats.

Vargas Island

Vargas Island has rugged uplands, sandy beaches, and abundant marine life. Access is by boat, kayak, or floatplane. Ahous Bay, the largest beach, is home to a sub-species of gray wolf.

Eagle Aerie Gallery

The tranquil cedar-planked Eagle Aerie Gallery in Tofino is a hand-hewn longhouse with a carved and painted housefront traditional to the local First Nations people. Internationally acclaimed Tsimshian printmaker Roy Henry Vickers is the gallerist, and his artwork is also on sale here *(below)*.

Pacific Rim National Park Reserve of Canada

World-famous area for whale-watching, the 81-mi- (130-km-) long park is made up of three distinct areas: Long Beach, the West Coast Trail, and the Broken Group Islands *(see p101)*.

Wild Pacific Trail

This breathtaking 10-16-km) trail runs along-the Pacific Ocean through coastal rainforest, to the tip of the Ucluelet peninsula to the Pacific Rim National Park. Hikers are surrounded by stands of conifers in the largest lowland temperate rainforest on earth.

Ucluelet

This small town is the gateway to multiple outdoor activities on both land and water. Avid fishers flock here for steelhead, sturgeon, halibut, and Pacific and fresh-water salmon. The climate is temperate, with 328 frost-free days a year.

West Coast Trail

The West Coast Trail is a challenging 46-mi (75-km) hike along a historic trail built to aid the rescue of shipwrecked mariners. The trail hugs the shoreline where approximately 65 ships met their demise. Rocky headlands along the trail are dotted with caves, arches, and waterfalls.

Gray Whales

Each year, an estimated 22,000 gray whales migrate past the Vancouver Island coast around Long Beach. They're on an 11,000-mi (17,700-km) round trip, migrating south from the Arctic to their breeding grounds off southern California and Mexico from December to early February, and returning north from March through May.

Reservations and permits are required for the West Coast Trail, which can be hiked in part or full (seven days); call 250 387 1642

Whistler

The 75-mi (120-km) drive to Whistler from Vancouver reveals stunning scenery, a combination of Howe Sound's sparkling blue waters and the majestic snow-covered Coast Mountain range. Welcoming more than two million visitors each year, the side-by-side peaks of Whistler and Blackcomb mountains are magnificent. A year-round resort, Whistler continues to grow as the 2010 Olympic and Paralympic Winter Games approach. The resort is known for its exemplary accommodations and over 90 restaurants and 200 shops. Yet it still preserves natural enclaves of forests and five lakes.

Chalet, Upper Village

🍴 Horstman Hut is the uppermost eatery in the area, sitting at 7,494 ft (2,284 m) on Blackcomb Mountain.

💰 Canada's resort tax can take a bite out of your wallet. You may be eligible for a rebate *(see p112)*.

For free information, visit the Whistler Visitor Information Centre, 201-4230 Gateway Dr; 604 932 5922, ext 17.

Take warm clothing when heading up the mountains, even in summer.

• Map F1
• www.mywhistler.com
• Whistler Activity and Information Centre, 4010 Whistler Way, 604 938 2769 or 1 877 991 9988
• Whistler Central Reservations: 604 664 5625 or 1 800 944 7853

Top 10 Features

1. Whistler Mountain
2. Blackcomb Mountain
3. Whistler Village
4. Alta Lake
5. Upper Village
6. Valley Trail
7. Fairmont Chateau Whistler
8. Green Lake
9. Creekside
10. Village North

1 Whistler Mountain

Skiers and snowboarders enjoy 3,557 acres (1,440 ha) of impressive terrain with over 100 marked trails *(center)*. Whistler Village Gondola offers superb views of Whistler Valley during the 20-minute ride to the top. Mountain biking and alpine hiking are exceptional summer activities. Mountain-top restaurants offer everything from snacks to fine dining.

2 Blackcomb Mountain

Blackcomb, nicknamed the "Mile High Mountain," towers over Whistler resort at an elevation of 7,494 ft (2,284 m). Skiers and snowboarders ride to more than 100 marked runs from three bases. In summer, a sightseeing trip to Horstman Glacier is not to be missed. Or take advantage of the glacier's superb summer skiing and snowboarding.

3 Whistler Village

This pedestrian-only Alpine-style enclave ringed by shops, hotels, and restaurants *(below)* provides ski-in, ski-out access to Whistler Mountain. It's busy round the clock with skiers and boarders heading to the mountain, diners on patios, and late-night clubgoers.

Leave yourself plenty of time for the scenic drive to Whistler; construction delays are likely before the 2010 Winter Olympi

Alta Lake
1 Alta Lake was once home to Rainbow Lodge, Whistler's first resort. Traces of the lodge remain at Rainbow Park *(above)*, a delightful picnic spot. Explore the lake's perimeter along the paved Valley Trail, or swim, wind surf, or canoe.

Green Lake
8 A glacial gem with crystal clear water courtesy of mountain melt, Green Lake is truly green. It is a firm favorite of canoeists, with views taking in some of the area's highest peaks, including massive Mount Currie.

Creekside
9 A recent multi-million dollar investment has transformed this activity center, providing glamorous hotels and a mini-mall. Skiers can access Whistler Mountain from this historic base at the Creekside Gondola.

Upper Village
5 Nestled at the base of Blackcomb Mountain, the Upper Village offers easy access to the slopes. The ski-in, ski-out luxury hotels, award-winning restaurants, and quality shops here are unsurpassed. The huge Day Lot adjacent to the village offers free parking.

Valley Trail
6 This 12-mi (20-km) Valley Trail attracts walkers, cyclists, and in-line skaters. It leads past Lost Lake, Rainbow Park, and Alta, Nita, and Alpha lakes, through stands of trees fringing residential areas. In winter, the Lost Lake loop is dedicated to cross-country skiing.

Fairmont Chateau Whistler
7 Whistler's grand dame *(above)* reigns over the valley from the Upper Village. The antique furnishings, gold-leaf ceiling painting, and Canadian art in the lobby of this chateau-style hotel make it well worth a visit. The opulent Mallard Bar has a popular heated patio.

Village North
10 Construction of Village North followed that of Upper Village, with the added attractions of vehicle access, a shopping mall complete with The Marketplace – one of the resort's best grocery stores – cafés, restaurants, and intriguing shops.

Whistler Transit
A free shuttle service runs every 20 to 30 minutes between village hotels and condos to the ski slopes. WAVE, the municipal bus service, transports visitors to and from the villages and around the town. For a taxi, call 604 932 3333.

For a glimpse into Whistler's pioneer history, visit Whistler Museum & Archives, 4329 Main St, Village North; call 604 932 2019

Left **Fairmont Chateau Whistler Golf Course** Right **Snowboarding, Blackcomb Mountain**

TOP 10 Fun Things to Do in Whistler

1 Skiing
Whistler and Blackcomb cater to all ages and levels of skiers. With over 30 ft (10 m) of snow fall yearly, boosted by snowmaking, the winter season provides over 200 runs. Summer skiing on Blackcomb's glacier.

2 Golf
Known as the "Big Four," Whistler's four golf courses take advantage of their mountain settings, with lakes, creeks, rolling greens, and mountain views. Golfers are pampered with deluxe facilities and fine dining. ◈ *Whistler Central Reservations: 1 800 944 7853*

Black bear cub

3 Dog Sledding
The distinctly northern activity of dog sledding, with energetic huskies eager to pull their sleds through the backcountry, is suitable for both adults and kids who enjoy mushing seven-dog teams. An easy, off-road adventure.
◈ *Cougar Mountain: 1 888 297 2222*

4 Snowmobiling and Snowcat Tours
Speedy snowmobiles are an exhilarating way to see Blackcomb Mountain, or try the more sedate, heated Snowcat. A pleasant dinner at the alpine Crystal Hut can be added. ◈ *Canadian Snowmobile Adventures: 604 938 1616*

5 Snowboarding
Annual upgrades at the thrilling terrain parks ensure bigger and better rails and pipes for the advanced. Well-designed novice areas also.

6 Bear Watching
An intimate, respectful view of Whistler's black bears is offered on tours led by local bear researcher Michael Allen. Fifty or so bears live in the area's old-growth forests, feeding on the grassy mountain slopes and foraging for berries. Allen's tours provide an up-close look at bear habits and habitats suitable for all ages.

7 Mountain Biking
Free-flowing runs as well as technically demanding trails groomed to perfection. Practice comes easy at the Mountain Bike Park, with its three Skills Centres, and jumps and learning tools for all levels.

Mountain biker, Whistler Mountain

Whistler and Blackcomb's winter ski season runs from late November to late April

Top 10 Best Whistler Festivals

Whistler's Pioneers

Before Whistler Valley became a ski destination, the area was a magnet for explorers, miners, loggers, and pioneer entrepreneurs such as Alex and Myrtle Philip. The young American couple arrived in 1912, and two years later opened a fishing lodge on Alta Lake. Rainbow Lodge was soon BC's premiere resort destination, with visitors arriving on the now defunct Pacific Great Eastern Railway. The lodge burned down in 1977, but one of Rainbow Park's original guest log cabins and a replica of Alex's romantic Bridge of Sighs mark where it once stood.

Rainbow Lodge
The resort's main lodge was built from handcut and peeled logs. By its peak, 45 buildings had been constructed. Only four original cabins remain.

Alpine Sightseeing

Snowy peaks, glaciers, and mpses of Whistler's namesake, hoary marmot, or "whistler," ke summer hikes memorable. istler's 30 mi (48 km) of marked ls are easy to follow. Refresh he Roundhouse Lodge. The en-chair ascent to Horstman cier *(see p28)* is thrilling.

Adventure Zone

Parents and children play ether in the exciting Blackcomb se Adventure Zone in the Upper age. Not to be missed is the d-sized Westcoaster Luge

track snaking down the mountain. Other activities include the climbing center, bungee ride, and Spin Cycle, an astronaut-inspired ride.

10 Canoeing and Whitewater Rafting

Resort pioneer Alex Philip began the canoeing craze on picturesque Alta Lake. It's still a low-key way to spend a hot summer day. Canoe rentals and guided tours available. For a faster pace, whitewater raft the Green, Birkenhead, and Elaho rivers. ◈ *Canoeing: Whistler Outdoor Experience: 604 932 3389 • Whistler River Adventures: 604 932 3532*

For details on activities at Whistler and Blackcomb, including bear watching, call 1 800 766 0449 or visit www.whistlerblackcomb.com

31

Left **Chinese Cultural Centre Museum & Archives** Right **Vancouver Museum**

Museums & Art Galleries

1 UBC Museum of Anthropology

Situated on cliffs overlooking Burrard Inlet, this airy museum houses over 500,000 ethnographic and archaeological objects from around the world, with emphasis on coastal First Nations.
* 6393 NW Marine Dr
* Map A2 • 604 822 5087
* Open 11am–9pm Tue, 11–5pm Wed–Sun
* Adm

The Raven and the First Men, **UBC Museum of Anthropology**

2 Vancouver Art Gallery

The Vancouver Art Gallery's growing collection is rich in historic and contemporary works by BC and international artists, including the world's largest grouping of Emily Carr pieces. The splendid *fin-de-siècle* exhibition hall hosts traveling exhibits *(see pp18–19)*.

3 Vancouver Police Centennial Museum

An intriguing glimpse into the dark world of crime and punishment in Vancouver's past. The 10,000 artifacts housed in the old Coroner's Court include confiscated weapons, counterfeit bills, and displays depicting scientific evidence. You may find yourself amid a gaggle of wide-eyed children, as school tours play an important part of programming. * 240 E Cordova St • 604 665 3346 • Open 9am–5pm Mon–Sat • Adm

4 Chinese Cultural Centre Museum and Archives

Part of the Chinese Cultural Centre, the museum and archives share traditional Chinese architecture. The collection tells of the Chinese community from the Cariboo Gold Rush of the 1860s to the settlement of Chinatown. The annex exhibits classical and contemporary Chinese art. * 555 Columbia St • Map M4 • 604 658 8880 • Open Tue–Sun 11am–5pm • Adm

5 Vancouver Museum

Permanent and short-term exhibits offer intimate looks at Vancouver's heritage. Hands-on exhibits, such as the 1950s soda shop, and a visit to the hippie era in Vancouver – complete with macramé clothes to try on – make recent history a delight *(see p79)*.

The Crab, by George Norris, **Vancouver Museum**

Previous pages **The Wickaninnish Inn near Long Beach, Vancouver Island**

6 Charles H. Scott Gallery

An adjunct to the Emily Carr Institute of Art and Design (see p21), the gallery has a mandate to promote visual education and dialogue. Shows feature innovative art of emerging and established artists, both local and international. ◎ 1399 Johnston St • Map H5 • 604 844 3809 • Open noon–5pm Mon–Fri, 10am–5pm Sat–Sun • Adm

7 BC Sports Hall of Fame and Museum

BC's sports achievements, including those of local heroes Terry Fox and his Marathon of Hope, and Rick Hansen's and his Man in Motion World Tour, are celebrated in 20,000 sq ft (1858 sq m) of gallery space. The Participation Gallery entices visitors to try pitching, sprinting, and rock climbing. ◎ 777 Pacific Blvd • Map L4–L5 • 604 687 5520 • Open 10am–5pm daily • Adm

8 Vancouver Maritime Museum

Exhibits of artifacts, models, vessels, and photos pay tribute to Canada's marine heritage. At the heart of the collection is the restored 104-ft (32-m) ketch St. Roch, the second ship to navigate the North West Passage, but the first to travel it from west to east (see p77).

Granville Island Museums

9 Granville Island Museums

These three museums are housed in one building. Anglers will revel in the Sport Fishing Museum's extensive display of reels, creels, and tied flies. The Model Train Museum has a large collection of tiny trains, displayed in dioramas of forests and canyons. The Model Ship Museum offers models of innumerable vessels, from barges and battleships to subs and sail boats (see p77).

10 Inuit Gallery

One of the region's most respected commercial galleries, showing an outstanding selection of Inuit and North West Coast Native sculpture, graphics, and jewelry. ◎ 206 Cambie St • Map L3 • 604 688 7323 • Open 10am–6pm Mon-Sat, 11am–5pm Sun

Left **Carved doors, Museum of Anthropology** Right **Kwakwaka'wakw totem pole, Thunderbird Park**

🔟 First Nations Art

1 'Ksan Mural

Five artists carved this red cedar frieze to illustrate Northwest Coast raven myths. The nine panels tell stories of how the Raven created the elements of the world through his mischievous activities. ✆ *1025 W Georgia St • Map K3*

2 The Jade Canoe

Haida artist Bill Reid's awe-inspiring bronze creation is the second casting of *The Black Canoe*. Thirteen creatures from Haida mythology paddle an imposing 20 ft (6 m) canoe.

The Jade Canoe, by Bill Reid

✆ *Vancouver International Airport • Map A2*

3 Inukshuk

Made by Alvin Kanak for Expo '86, the granite sculpture is an Inuit welcome figure, a traditional traveler's marker, although much larger than those found in the North. ✆ *English Bay Beach • Map G3*

4 Carved Doors

The entrance to UBC's Museum of Anthropology *(see p34)* is itself a work of art. Made of red cedar by four Gitxsan master carvers, the double doors convey a narrative from the Skeena River region. When closed, the images form the shape of a Northwest Coast bent box used for storage as well as burials.

5 Kwakwaka'wakw Totem Pole

Completed in 1999, this pole at Victoria's Royal British Columbia Museum *(see pp24–5)* provides a chance to see a powerful modern interpretation of traditional carving by two young Kwakwaka'wakw artists, Jonathan Henderson and Sean Wonnock. The pole features a mythical thunderbird on top of the tail of an orca.

6 Hetux

International travelers alighting at the Vancouver airport are greeted by *Hetux*, a huge birch-and-aluminum image suspended from the ceiling. Connie Watts combines animal forms as diverse as the mythical thunderbird with the hummingbird, wolf, and salmon to reflect the untamed spirit of her grandmother. ✆ *Vancouver International Airport • Map A2*

7 Thunderbird House Post

Tony Hunt's majestic thunderbird stands above a grizzly bear, which in turn holds a human being. The house post is a replica of one of a pair carved in the early 1900s by influential artist Charlie James. After 40 years in Stanley Park, the poles deteriorated, were restored, and moved indoors. Carver Tony Hunt re-created the colorful cedar pole now standing in the park's Totem Park *(see p9)*

Totem art represents family clans with figures such as eagles, frogs, ravens, orcas, and grizzly bears; mythical creatures are also common

8 Chief of the Undersea World

Orcas were still kept at the Vancouver Aquarium when Haida artist Bill Reid's sculpture was installed outside it, in 1984. Those orcas are since gone, but this 16-ft- (5-m-) tall bronze killer whale leaping into the air remains as a tribute to this West Coast creature. ◈ *Stanley Park • Map G1*

9 World's Tallest Freestanding Totem Pole

Raised in Beacon Hill Park *(see p96)* in 1956, the pole, by Kwakwaka'wakw chief Mungo Martin with David Martin and Henry Hunt, took six months to carve from a cedar nearly 128 ft (39 m) high. ◈ *Map Q6*

10 Coast Salish Welcome Figures

Two 17-ft- (5-m-) tall red cedar figures welcome travelers to the airport's Custom Hall in traditional Musqueam style. Northwest Coast artist Susan A. Point carved both from the same log. ◈ *Vancouver International Airport • Map A2*

Coast Salish welcome figures

Top 10 Public Artworks

1 Knife Edge
A Henry Moore monumental abstract sculpture. ◈ *Queen Elizabeth Park • Map B2*

2 Photo Session
Join Seward Johnson's family of bronze figures posing for a snapshot. ◈ *Queen Elizabeth Park • Map B2*

3 The Crab
George Norris's stylized stainless-steel crab. ◈ *1100 Chestnut St • Map G4*

4 Gate to the Pacific Northwest
Alan Chung Hung's sculpture invokes 18th-century navigation instruments. ◈ *Vanier Park • Map G4*

5 Primavera
Wooden butterflies convey transformation in this acrylic painting by Jack Shadbolt. ◈ *1075 W Georgia St • Map J3*

6 Salute to the Lions of Vancouver
Gathie Falk's steel lions line up with the Lions Gate Bridge and The Lions mountain. ◈ *999 Canada Place Way • Map L2*

7 Angel of Victory
Coeur de Lion MacCarthy's bronze angel lifts a World War I soldier heavenward. ◈ *601 W Cordova St • Map L3*

8 Street Light
Panels shadow images of historic events onto a walkway. ◈ *Marinaside Cres • Map K5*

9 Pendulum
A stunning seven-story pendulum, by Alan Storey. ◈ *885 W Georgia St • Map K3*

10 Cooper's Mews
Footsteps trigger sounds from Alan Storey's barrel-and-railtrack homage to the area's industrial past. ◈ *1033 Marinaside Cres • Map K5*

Vancouver & Victoria's Top 10

Left **Sunken Garden, Butchart Gardens** Right **Macaw parrots, Bloedel Floral Conservatory**

Parks & Gardens

1 Pacific Spirit Regional Park

This huge, diverse, park is located on a peninsula on Vancouver's west side. It supports pine forests as well as birch, alder, and cottonwood trees. Extensive trails lead across the peninsula from Point Grey to the Fraser River. The park's terrain includes beaches, bluffs overlooking the expansive Spanish Banks, and the ancient Camosun Bog (see p88).

2 David Lam Park

With a large expanse of open green space, the slightly rolling Yaletown park has private corners for sitting and relaxing, and a lovely decorative pool. The park's Asian influence is expressed in its floral plantings. Children's play area. ◎ Map J5

3 Queen Elizabeth Park

This lovely park in central Vancouver was once a stone quarry. The Quarry Garden is now its centerpiece. A small rose garden is planted with hardy varieties that blossom year-round. Rolling treed slopes are perfect for summer picnics (see p88).

4 Stanley Park

Cedar, hemlock, and fir are rainforest favorites in the park. Old-fashioned roses and lush hybrid rhododendrons share the park with cherry, magnolia, and dogwood trees, and a multitude of others. Park staff plant 350,000 annual flowers for year-round beauty (see pp8–11).

5 Bloedel Floral Conservatory

Visitors to Canada's first geodesic conservatory are enveloped by steamy air as they step into this dome filled with desert and tropical plants. The calls of free-flying birds add to the ambience.
◎ Queen Elizabeth Park, W 33rd Ave & Cambie St • Map B2 • 604 257 8570

6 Spanish Banks Beach Park

With the longest expanse of sandy beach in Vancouver, the park is shared by walkers, cyclists, picnickers, and families splashing in the tidal waters. ◎ Map A2

7 Dr. Sun Yat-Sen Classical Chinese Garden

This gem of a park in Chinatown reflects the serenity of a Ming Dynasty garden (see p63).

Dr. Sun Yat-Sen Classical Chinese Garden

Spanish Banks, beside Pacific Spirit Regional Park, is one of the best spots in the city to watch the sun set over the water

Camosun Bog, Pacific Spirit Regional Park

Top 10 BC Trees

1 Douglas Fir
The province's economy was built on the lumber from this imposing tree that grows as tall as 300 ft (90 m).

2 Yellow Cedar
Growing in colder elevations, its soft wood is the ideal choice for First Nations carvings.

3 Western Red Cedar
Dark, scale-like needles mark the down swept branches of this sometimes huge tree.

4 Hemlock
The most common tree on the West Coast, the hemlock is easily recognizable by its droopy top.

5 Sitka Spruce
The Carmanah Giant, a Sitka spruce found on Vancouver Island is, at 312 ft (95 m), the tallest recorded tree in Canada.

6 Arbutus
Peeling red-brown bark marks the arbutus, also known as the madrona, the only broad-leafed evergreen tree native to Canada.

7 Pine
Straight lodgepole and Ponderosa pines grow at higher elevations.

8 Dogwood
The white or pink flowers of the province's floral emblem bloom in spring.

9 Japanese Flowering Cherry
More than 19,000 of these exquisite blossoming trees line Vancouver city streets.

10 Maple
Canada's national tree grows in bigleaf, Douglas, and vine varieties. Bigleaf wood is used for First Nations canoe paddles.

8 Butchart Gardens
Starting in 1904, Mrs. Jenny Butchart created five spectacular gardens to beautify her huband's excavated limestone quarry on the outskirts of Victoria. Her first creation was the Japanese Garden. Next came the lush Sunken Garden. Some one million bedding plants blossom yearly, showcasing 700 plant varieties (see p101).

9 VanDusen Botanical Garden
The array of flowers, shrubs, and trees are unrivaled in Vancouver. Over 7,500 varieties of plants from six continents take advantage of the city's four distinct seasons. Rolling lawns, peaceful lakes, artistic rockwork, and forested pockets (see p88).

10 Vanier Park
English Bay is the backdrop for this expansive park near Granville Island. Largely treeless, the 37-acre (15-ha) area was named after Georges P. Vanier, governor general of Canada from 1959 to 1967. Kite-flyers delight in the open vista, their colorful kites dancing in the wind (see p78).

To avoid disappointment, book ahead for a spot at the VanDusen Botanical Garden's Festival of Lights in December

Left **Provence Marinaside** Right **Bacchus Restaurant**

🔟 Restaurants

1 Provence Marinaside
Dining at the wood tables amid the bright Mediterranean color scheme is a casual delight, with the food itself living up to fine dining. Fresh local seafood is featured, with a raw oyster bar and antipasti showcase. A sommelier helps out with the impressive wine list. Weekend brunches *(see p83)*.

2 CinCin Ristorante & Bar
The Mediterranean-inspired menu of this inviting space includes wood-fired pizzas and alder wood-grilled meat and fish. If you're not in a rush, order the melt-in-your-mouth free range chicken cooked under a brick in the wood-fired oven for 25 minutes. On the terrace, trees mute the hustle of the street below. Choose from 925 wines *(see p73)*.

CinCin Ristorante & Bar

3 Blue Water Café and Raw Bar
Exquisite wild seafood is served in a 100-year-old brick-and-beam warehouse. The decor is contemporary, the atmosphere friendly, and the kitchen serves mouthwatering delicacies such as Quadra Island honey mussel soup and seafood towers of fresh shellfish, sushi, and Dungeness crab. The Raw Bar is the domain of a master sushi chef. Superb champagne list *(see p83)*.

4 Il Giardino
Internationally known restaurateur and chef Umberto Menghi has re-created the mood and atmosphere of Tuscany. Menu choices satisfy with items such as *osso buco*, roasted pheasant, and flash-seared tuna. Follow up with one of the wonderful desserts, such as tiramisu or crème brûlée, all made in-house. An extensive wine list includes international and local vintages. In the summer, the exquisite garden patio is a favorite *(see p83)*.

5 Bacchus Restaurant
A pianist plays as diners savor the dishes created from locally sourced ingredients, including wild salmon, ranch venison, and rack of lamb. Gorgeously lush, Bacchus reeks of old-city money and attracts a clientele appreciative of its European-style setting European, California, and BC wines make up a noteworthy wine list *(see p73)*.

Blue Water Café and Raw Bar

West Coast cuisine highlights local seafood, meats, and produce, often incorporating ingredients unique to the region

Diva at the Met

Diva at the Met

6 Pacific Northwest dining with an international touch. Seating is on four tiers, beneath lofty ceilings. Stand-out dishes include slow-smoked Washington State duck and Alaskan black cod. The desserts tempt one to forgo an entrée. A sommelier helps choose from 550 selections (see p73).

Imperial Chinese Seafood Restaurant

7 This jewel of a restaurant offers Cantonese delicacies such as shark's fin soup, Peking duck, and sautéed lobster and crab. Lunch and dinner are served, but enticing *dim sum* appear only at lunch. Repeatedly named a Distinguished Restaurant of North America, the Imperial is buoyed by a bevy of Hong Kong-trained chefs (see p65).

Raincity Grill

8 White table-cloths, leather banquets, and wood floors make for casual, upscale dining. The menu is seasonal: game in winter gives way to fish choices in summer. West Coast wines from California to BC are featured (see p73).

Cioppino's Mediterranean Grill

9 Inventive *cucina*-style dishes are made with fresh vegetables, olive oil, and low-fat cream sauces for a pleasing meal that is easy on the waistline. Or choose the juicy Black Angus beef with calamari, lobster, and escargot. A patio and excellent wine list round out the experience (see p83).

C Restaurant

10 The best of contemporary regional fish dishes are featured at this sleek waterfront restaurant. Try incomparable Kagan Bay scallops or Nordic spirit sablefish to get into the BC spirit. Chef Robert Clark has been voted one of the best in Canada (see p83).

*Early-bird **prix fixe** menus offer economy and variety at some restaurants; call ahead for details*

Left **Queen Elizabeth Theatre & Vancouver Playhouse** Right **BC Place**

TOP 10 Entertainment Venues

1 Queen Elizabeth Theatre & Vancouver Playhouse

Home to the Vancouver Opera and Ballet BC, and hosting many guest artists, the Queen Elizabeth Theatre is located in a 1960s-built, Modernist venue. Adjacent to this theater, in an urbane yet cozy 672-seat space, is the Vancouver Playhouse Theatre Company, which features classics by Shakespeare, Shaw, and others, along with modern US and Canadian plays. ◈ *Hamilton at Dunsmuir sts* • *Map L4* • *604 665 3050* • *www.city.vancouver.bc.ca/theatres*

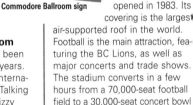

Commodore Ballroom sign

2 Commodore Ballroom

The Commodore has been around for more than 75 years. Its eclectic national and international acts have included Talking Heads, Tina Turner, and Dizzy Gillespie, as well as Canada's hottest bands and solo artists, and world music performers. Tickets required *(see p74)*.

3 Stanley Theatre

This 1930s movie house was restored to its former elegance in 1998. It is now home to musicals, classical plays, and comedies. The Stanley is one of the city's most nostalgic venues, a classic favorite remembered fondly by many oldtimers. ◈ *2750 Granville St* • *Map B2* • *604 687 1644* • *www.artsclub.com*

4 General Motors (GM) Place

This huge venue is home to the Vancouver Canucks National Hockey League team. The stadium is also one of the busiest entertainment venues in North America: since 1995, the venue has hosted some 170 concerts and events each year. ◈ *Pacific Blvd N at Abbott St* • *Map L4* • *604 899 7889* • *www.canucks.com/gm*

5 BC Place

A Vancouver landmark with its white-domed roof, this stadium opened in 1983. Its covering is the largest air-supported roof in the world. Football is the main attraction, featuring the BC Lions, as well as major concerts and trade shows. The stadium converts in a few hours from a 70,000-seat football field to a 30,000-seat concert bowl ◈ *777 Pacific Blvd* • *Map L4–L5* • *604 669 2300* • *www.bcplacestadium.com*

6 Vancouver East Cultural Centre

Canadian and international theater and dance, Baroque opera, music from string quartets to bluegrass, and family programs are all presented in this renovated 1909 Methodist church. Folksy with an avant-garde twist best describes the shows in this casual, small-theater setting. ◈ *1895 Venables St* • *Map B2* • *604 251 1363* • *www.vecc.bc.ca*

Vancouver & Victoria's Top 10

Orpheum Theatre

7 Restored to Baroque grandeur, the Orpheum is a lush, former Vaudeville palace built in 1926. Vancouver-born Hollywood star Yvonne de Carlo was an usherette here briefly in the late 1930s. Vancouver Symphony Orchestra and choral concerts, rock shows, and other quality musical events are performed here in the acoustically upgraded space. ✆ *884 Granville St • Map K4 • 604 665 3050 • www.city.vancouver.bc.ca/theatres*

Firehall Arts Centre

8 This heritage fire station, circa 1906, is now an innovative Gastown theater. Modern plays, many by home-grown talents, reflect cultural diversity through comedy and drama. The 175-seat studio theater includes an outdoor stage. A cozy, licensed lounge offers a chance to mix with local theater-goers. ✆ *280 E Cordova St • Map M4 • 604 689 0926 • www.firehallartscentre.ca*

Granville Island Stage/ New Revue Stage

9 The Arts Club's 480-seat Granville Island Stage, and 220-seat New Revue Stage across the alley, prove theater doesn't have to be formal. Comedies and dramas

Orpheum Theatre

with a light touch are featured at the former, while daring Vancouver TheatreSports League improvisation shows fill the latter. ✆ *Granville Island Stage: 1585 Johnston St, 604 687 1644; TheatreSports League, 1601 Johnston St, 604 738 7013 • Map H5 • www.artsclub.com*

Chan Centre for the Performing Arts

10 In this striking, cylindrical, three-venue center music is performed in the glorious 1,200-seat Chan Shun Concert Hall, whose adjustable acoustic canopy allows all types of music to sound their best. A small, experimental theater and a cinema round out the entertainment venues. ✆ *6265 Crescent Rd, University of British Columbia • Map A2 • 604 822 9197 • www.chancentre.com*

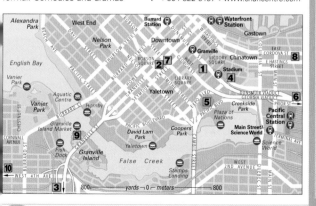

Left **Bard on the Beach** Right **Vancouver Pride Festival parade**

TOP 10 Festivals & Events

1 Bard on the Beach Shakespeare Festival

Bard on the Beach, Western Canada's largest professional Shakespeare festival, presents works by the Bard, and related events. English Bay forms the backdrop for the open-air stages. ◈ Vanier Park • Map G4 • Jun–late Sep • 604 737 0559

2 Alcan Canadian International Dragon Boat Festival

Over 2,500 paddlers from around the world gather for a weekend of exhilarating fun. There's more to do than just watch the races. Food, exhibits, and entertainment abound. Admission to Science World is included in the ticket price. ◈ False Creek • mid-Jun • 604 688 2382

Alcan Dragon Boat Festival

3 HSBC Celebration of Light

The night skies fill with spectacular fireworks, accompanied by broadcasted music, as three countries compete to win top bragging rights. Huge crowds flock to English Bay, Vanier Park, Kitsilano, Jericho, and West Vancouver beaches, so go early to snag a good spot, and bring a blanket to sit on. ◈ Jul & Aug

4 Vancouver Pride Festival

For two weeks, gays and friends of gays gather in the city's West End to celebrate diversity. The festival is a bevy of picnics, dances, cruises, breakfasts, and a grand finale parade and beach-side party, with thousands in attendance. ◈ late Jul–early Aug • 604 687 0955

5 Festival Vancouver

A sophisticated mix of Canadian and international classical, choral, jazz, and world musicians make this two-week event a perfect fit with Vancouver's urbane yet relaxed atmosphere. Held at various venues around the city, including UBC's First Nations longhouse; some performances and educational events are free. ◈ early Aug • 604 688 1152

Fireworks, HSBC Celebration of Light

For tickets to many of Vancouver's events and festivals, contact Ticketmaster 604 280 4444, www.ticketmaster.ca

6 Vancouver International Film Festival

Eclectic yet accessible programming draws over 150,000 people. A strong showing of films from Canada and the Pacific Rim.
🔊 *early Oct • 604 685 0260*

7 Vancouver International Jazz Festival

Jazz in every imaginable style and all its dimensions, from upwardly mobile performers to big names, is presented in some 400 concerts at various venues around town. Wraps up with an outdoor multi-stage free weekend.
🔊 *late Jun–early Jul • 604 872 5200*

8 Vancouver International Writers & Readers Festival

International and Canadian writers attract throngs of readers to forums, readings, and literary cabarets in English and French. Writers stay on the festival site, so there's a good chance you'll see and even chat to a celebrity author. 🔊 *Granville Island • late Oct • 604 681 6330*

9 Vancouver Folk Music Festival

Canadian and international performers play rain or shine on open-air stages. The waterside park becomes its own township as 25,000 folk music fanatics settle in for three evenings and two full days of non-stop music and good vibrations. 🔊 *Jericho Beach Park • mid-Jul • 604 602 9798*

10 Vancouver International Comedy Festival

Generous doses of stand-up, burlesque, sketch comedy, improvisation, and free street performances by top Canadian and international comedians.
🔊 *mid-Oct • 604 683 0883*

Top 10 Performing Groups

1 Firehall Arts Centre
Entertaining shows with a multi-cultural twist *(see p43)*.

2 Ballet British Columbia
World-class ballet under bold leadership. 🔊 *604 280 3311*

3 The Playhouse Theatre Company
Modern and classical plays, including Canadian works.
🔊 *604 873 3311*

4 Vancouver Opera Company
Grand-scale productions with ravishing Canadian and international voices. Traditional and contemporary pieces. 🔊 *604 683 0222*

5 Vancouver Symphony Orchestra
World-class orchestral music, often with international guest artists. 🔊 *604 280 3311*

6 Early Music Vancouver
Varied concerts of works by Medieval to late-Romantic composers. 🔊 *604 732 1610*

7 Arts Club Theatre Company
Contemporary drama at Granville Island Stage and the Stanley Theatre. 🔊 *604 280 3311*

8 Vancouver Theatresports League
Hilarious improv-based comedy and parody at Granville Island's New Revue Stage. 🔊 *604 738 7013*

9 Kokoro Dance Company
Distorted movement and great intensity characterize Kokoro's *butoh*, a postwar Japanese dance form. 🔊 *604 662 7441*

10 Hoarse Raven Theatre
Enjoy a delightful romp at long-running *Tony n' Tina's Wedding*. 🔊 *604 258 4079*

Left **Science World** Right **Sea otter, Vancouver Aquarium**

Children's Attractions

1 Science World
Kids can get involved in the displays at this hands-on discovery center and they won't even know they're learning something. A good rainy day diversion, Science World also has birthday packages, and the Alcan OMNIMAX Theatre *(see pp22–3)*.

2 Miniature Railway & Children's Farmyard
Stanley Park's miniature railway makes a 15-minute excursion through the forest. At the Children's Farmyard, get up close to goats, sheep, pigs, and ponies, as

Miniature Railway locomotive

well as more exotic beasts. There's plenty to do for free, too. Second Beach has a play area, swimming pool, and beach.
⊛ *Stanley Park • Map G1 • 604 257 8531 • Open year-round; hrs vary • Adm • www.parks.vancouver.bc.ca*

3 Capilano Suspension Bridge
Walk the swaying bridge, then climb Treetops Adventure's boardwalks and platforms perched high in the forest *(see pp14–15)*.

4 CN IMAX Theatre
Kids will feel like they're in the middle of the action with this screen wide enough to hold a life-size image of a whale *(see p13)*.

5 Vancouver Aquarium
Canada's largest aquarium introduces kids to everything from eels and octopuses to tropical fish in re-created natural habitats. Naturalists are on hand to answer questions. Special events for kids include sleepovers with the whales *(see pp10–11)*.

6 Richmond Nature Park
Even young children will be able to navigate the 3 miles (5 km) of well-groomed trails to spy turtles, frogs, hummingbirds, deer, or coyote around the bog, pond, and forest. The trail circling the pond is wheelchair accessible. The Nature House features interpretive exhibits, and special events include the popular Slugfest.
⊛ *11851 Westminster Hwy, Richmond • Map B3 • 604 718 6188 • Open 9am–5pm daily • Adm by donation*

Capilano Suspension Bridge

➔ *CN IMAX Theatre showings range from nature documentaries to animated features to remastered Hollywood blockbusters*

Skyride, Grouse Mountain

7 Grouse Mountain

Grouse offers more than just skiing and snowboarding. Summer family activities include hiking, paragliding, guided eco-walks, or simply riding the Skyride to the top. At the Refuge for Endangered Wildlife, see peregrine falcons, gray wolves, and grizzlies. Loggers throw axes and roll logs at the lumberjack show *(see p86)*.

8 H.R. MacMillan Space Centre

Touch a moon rock, morph into an alien, or climb aboard a spacecraft and let the motion simulator replicate the feeling of space travel. Laser and star shows *(see p78)*.

9 Playland & the Pacific National Exhibition

Playland has rides for all ages, including its famed wooden roller coaster, plus a climbing wall, minigolf, midway games, and cotton candy. The Pacific National Exhibition runs mid-August to September, with animals, entertainment, and demolition derbies. ✆ 2901 E Hastings St • Map B2 • 604 253 2311 • Open Jun–Sep: daily; Apr–May: Sat & Sun; hrs vary • Adm • www.pne.ca

10 Maplewood Farm

Kids enjoy pony rides, sheep shearing, cow milking, and mingling with the animals at this farm. Picnic area, greenhouse, and aviary, too. ✆ 405 Seymour River Pl, N Vancouver • Map C1 • 604 929 5610

Top 10 Places to Eat with Kids

1 Old Spaghetti Factory
Pastas and more in a memorabilia-filled warehouse. ✆ 53 Water St • 604 684 1288

2 White Spot
Classic burgers, fries, and Pirate Packs, as well as healthier choices. ✆ 580 W Georgia St • 604 662 3066

3 Sophie's Cosmic Café
Fun 1950s decor with booths, big portions of comfort food, weekend lineups. ✆ 2095 W 4th Ave • 604 732 6810

4 Sha Lin Noodle House
Cheap and yummy noodles, made before your eyes. ✆ 548 W Broadway • 604 873 1816

5 Café Deux Soleil
Where hip young vegetarian families meet. Toddlers' play area. ✆ 2096 Commercial Dr • 604 254 1195

6 The Cat's Meow
Unfussy lunch spot near Granville Island's Kids Market. ✆ 1540 Old Bridge St • 604 647 2287

7 Hon's Wun-Tun House
Potstickers, soup, *dim sum*, quick service in a lively informal atmosphere. ✆ 1339 Robson St • 604 685 0871

8 Earl's
Dishes for everyone, from pizza to fine dinners. ✆ 1185 Robson St • 604 669 0020

9 Boathouse
Relaxed West Coast cuisine, children's menu, great view from the patio. ✆ 1795 Beach Ave • 604 669 2225

10 Topanga Café
A laid-back Vancouver favorite serving California-style Mexican food from a menu that children can have fun coloring. ✆ 2904 W 4th Ave • 604 733 3713

Several of the kids-friendly restaurants listed have multiple locations; check the phone book

Left **Seawall, English Bay** Right **Snowboarder, Cypress Provincial Park**

Great Outdoor Places

1 English Bay

This beautiful bay is a popular West End attraction. On New Year's Day it hosts the polar bear swim, when thousands of swimmers brave the cold waters. More popular is walking the seawall that runs beside the bay into Stanley Park, fueled with caffeine or ice cream from nearby Davie and Denman street cafés *(see p8)*.

2 Lighthouse Park

Park in the convenient lot or hop off the bus and enjoy a fairly easy walk though West Vancouver's 500-year-old forest to the boulder-lined shore, and the 1912 Point Atkinson Light-

Lighthouse, Lighthouse Park

house. The old-growth forest was slated to be felled to provide fuel for the lighthouse and its steam fog alarm. Luckily, it was never logged. Six miles (9.5 km) of trails provide day hikes through this entirely natural park, with its native trees and plants *(see p88)*.

3 Jericho Beach

This family-friendly park has an outdoor shower and changing rooms for freshening up after a day splashing in the water. Picnics on the beach are a favorite pastime. To take advantage of Pacific breezes, rent a windsurfer. Lessons are available for beginners to advanced. ⊗ *Map A1* • *Windsure Windsurfing: 604 224 0615*

4 Cypress Provincial Park

Cypress Mountain, one of the park's several peaks, is the biggest alpine ski and snowboarding area on the North Shore. In summer, activities include mountain biking, hiking, and wilderness camping in the park's rugged backcountry areas.
⊗ *Map A1* • *604 926 5612*

5 Grouse Mountain

The gondola ride to the summit provides thrilling views of the city and beyond. Skiing and snowboarding are guaranteed in winter, courtesy of snowmakers. Sightseeing and lots of activities in the summer *(see p86)*.

6 Kitsilano Beach and Park

"Kits" Park is connected by a tree-lined walk to the beach, favored by swimsuit-clad volleyball players and sunbathers. Busy Olympic-size Kitsilano Pool overlooks the beach. ⊗ *Map B2* • *Kitsilano Pool: 604 731 0011*

Kitsilano Beach

A seawall extends from west of Jericho Beach through Kitsilano and Vanier parks (see p78) to Granville Island (see pp20–21) and beyond

7 Wreck Beach

Getting down to Wreck Beach is easy, via a steep trail leading from SW Marine Drive on the UBC campus (see p85). The hard part is the climb back up from this clothing-optional beach. Beware: ogglers on the beach are conspicuous. There are spectacular views across the Strait of Georgia toward Vancouver Island (see p53).

8 Mount Seymour Provincial Park

Drive to the top of Mount Seymour for glimpses of deer and bears, and for views of Deep Cove and Indian Arm. The park, on the eastern end of the Coast Mountain range, is popular in winter, with gentle slopes for beginners as well as challenges for more advanced skiers and snowboarders. Hiking is a summer activity. The park encompasses Mount Seymour, Mount Elsay, and Mount Bishop. Map C1 • 604 986 2261

9 Beacon Hill Park

Since 1858, Beacon Hill Park has been the queen of Victoria's open-air spaces. Wooden bridges over the stream, petting zoo, and English-style rose garden add charm to the peaceful setting. Views of the Strait of Juan de Fuca from some points in the 62-acre (25-ha) park. Visitors can walk, bird-watch, ride horses, and picnic on the beach (see p96).

10 Cathedral Grove

The grove, located in MacMillan Provincial Park on Vancouver Island, provides an awe-inspiring look at a virgin coastal forest. Giant, ancient Douglas-fir trees share the forest with stands of hemlock and Western red cedar. Loop trails are located on either side of Hwy 4. Scenic Cameron Lake is nearby. Map C4

Top 10 Outdoor Activities

1 Cycling
Stanley Park's seawall (see p8) has a dedicated bike lane. Spokes Bicycle Rentals, 1798 W Georgia St • 604 688 5141

2 Sailing
English Bay and Vancouver's outer harbor beckon. Simplicity Sailing Charters • 604 765 0074

3 Rock Climbing
Over 1,000 routes on the Squamish Chief make it a top climbing destination (see p89).

4 Skiing & Snowboarding
Whistler-Blackcomb is one of the top resorts in North America (see pp28–31).

5 Hiking
Completing the 2-mile (3-km) Grouse Grind wins you bragging rights (see p86).

6 Canoeing & Kayaking
Vancouver and Gulf Island canoeing and kayaking take little training. Lotus Land Tours • 604 684 4922

7 Golfing
Golden Ears mountains are the backdrop for a championship course. Newlands Golf & Country Club, 21025 48th Ave, Langley • 604 533 3288

8 In-line Skating
Stanley Park's seawall (see p8) makes for a satisfyingly long skate. Bayshore Rentals, 745 Denman St • 604 688 2453

9 Snowshoeing
Take a few minutes to master the skill, then enjoy the pristine wilderness. Cypress Mountain • 604 926 5612

10 Whale-Watching
Don a sweater and waterproof jacket, bring your binoculars, and watch the majestic orcas (see p109).

Left **AuBAR** Right **Sonar**

🔟 Bars & Clubs

1 AuBAR Nightclub

An upscale feel is created by the polished decor, complete with candles dotting the tables of the intimate seating areas. Lofty 22-ft (7-m) ceilings give an open feel to the dance floor. Friday night features top DJs spinning hip-hop and R&B, while Saturday nights percolate with Top 40s music. Plush seating in the lounge is also inviting. High-rollers drink Courvoisier and Hennessey. Fruity martinis such as Carmel Apple, Passion, and Starburst are favorites. This is definitely a see-and-be-seen type of place. You might even spot a Hollywood celebrity or two in the crowd. Dress code enforced. *(see p74).*

ginger 62 sign

2 ginger 62

Action in this self-styled "cocktail den and kitchen" starts at 8pm every night of the week. The atmosphere of the bar, with its dance floor, lounge, and more intimate Red Room, is a mix of 1960s and Asian inspirations. Reservations are a must for a seat at the cool white-and-red banquets. Live music and hot DJs – spinning hip-hop, R&B, club tracks, house, and more – are boosted by yummy Asian-influenced tapas. The hip crowd also loves its martinis and cocktails, with names like Frank & Dean and Ginger Not Marianne *(see p74).*

3 Sonar

This sexy and casual Gastown club accommodates crowds of 500 and more. Red brick arches lead from the front lounge into a variety of areas, including a stand-up bar and black leather banquets. Hip-hop, Top 40, and funk are at home here, with Sonic Saturdays guided by DJs, and alternative and electronic music on Sunday night *(see p64).*

4 AFTERglow Lounge

An intimate, 50-seat area adjacent to glowbal grill & satay bar *(see p83),* this lounge is dark, smooth, and mellow. The crowd looks good, the energy is positive, and there's a tasting-style satay menu. More than 20 wines are offered by the glass, plus yummy martinis *(see p82).*

5 Commodore Ballroom

Opened in 1926, this club has weathered many musical eras. Catch one of the many great acts or, on Tuesday nights, test out the room's bouncy sprung floor as you dance to disco music or party at one of the ample tables along the sides. Updated, and always on the cutting edge of music, the Commodore lives on as the city's great-grandfather of clubs *(see p74).*

The 12-route NightBus service runs every 30 minutes nightly to 3am; route info: TransLink, 604 953 3333 or www.translink.bc.ca

6 Richard's on Richards

The granddaddy of local clubs is still going strong. Always in tune with the times, the club presents ticketed live shows by top rock and pop musicians from 7pm to 10pm. Then it swings open its doors for a free-for-all, as the DJ spins op 40 hits for those grooving on the spacious dance floor. Theme nights, too *(see p82)*.

ar, Richard's on Richards

7 Caprice Nightclub & Lounge

Clean, lean, and modern, this cavernous nightclub has a dance floor for 400. The music is eclectic, with dee-jayed retro classics and R&B. All-request Top 40 is featured on alternating nights. The lounge, with a separate entrance, is a more intimate space, with its warming fireplace *(see p74)*.

8 SkyBar

A three-level complex with a Miami feel, where the well-heeled downtown crowd lets loose after a hard-working week. On the first floor is a martini bar, on the second, a large dance floor, and on the rooftop, a restaurant *(see p74)*.

9 The Irish Heather

This gastro-pub serves up good food in a casual and friendly pub setting. Shebeen, a whiskey house with a fantastic selection of single malts, bourbon, rye, scotch, and whiskey, is located in a renovated 19th-century coach house across the private courtyard *(see p64)*.

10 Crush Champagne Lounge

A fashionable lounge with a small dance floor. Eclectic entertainment adds to the energy of this casual, upbeat spot. Known for its wine list, Crush also offers all the usual refreshments, including champagne cocktails using fresh fruit purée. Jazz and classic lounge selections, R&B and soul *(see p74)*.

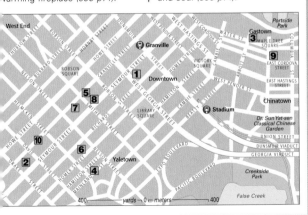

Buy tickets at the door, or at Ticketmaster outlets or online at www.ticketmaster.ca; call 604 280 4444 to charge by phone

51

Left **Patio, Fountainhead Pub** Right **Little Sister's sign**

Gay & Lesbian Hangouts

1 The Davie Village

Davie Village, with its fuchsia bus shelters and trash bins, is Vancouver's gay 'hood. Located in the West End between Burrard and Jervis streets, it's a 24-hour strip with cafés, myriad shops, including sex shops, clubs, restaurants for all budgets, and bars. The Centre, at 1170 Bute Street, provides health and social services to the community. ◎ *Map H4*

2 Fountainhead Pub

With its excellent selection of lagers on tap and appetizing menu, the Fountainhead Pub is a good first stop when hitting Davie Village. As a neighborhood sports bar, it's a great place to watch sports play-offs on TV. The patio is a prime spot for people-watching in the thick of the Village. ◎ *1025 Davie St • Map J4 • 604 687 2222*

Davie Village street banners

3 Little Sister's Book & Art Emporium

If there is an anchor to Vancouver gay community, Little Sister's is i More than a bookstore, it's a long standing institution that has taken Canada Customs to the Supreme Court of Canada i its fight for freedom from censorship. Good selection of literature, event tickets, gift items, clothing, DVDs, an play things. ◎ *123 Davie St • Map H3 • 604 669 1753*

4 Lick

Lick describes itself as Vancouver only "all-girl-operate underground queer night club." Welcoming everyone, the club has a great sound system, with harder core tech night on Thursdays. In a complex with three other bars, all gay-friendly. ◎ *455 Abbott St • Map L4 • 604 685 7777*

5 English Bay

Adorned with Pride flags in the summer, English Bay is the destination for those with coffees to-go from nearby cafés. Grab a park bench or a spot on the sandy beach and watch the world go by Or enjoy the vista from one of the bars and restaurants along the waterfront. In the heat of summe English Bay sizzles with skin and buff bods. It's also a great place to swim and suntan *(see p48)*.

English Bay

The Centre provides referrals, counseling, a library, and various programs; call 604 684 5307 or visit www.lgtbcentrevancouver.com

Celebrities

6 Celebrities
Brilliant lighting and visuals, state-of-the-art sound, and the city's hottest DJs and performers get the crowd – gay, straight, bi, and curious – moving. ◈ 1022 Davie St • Map J4 • 604 681 6180

7 Delaney's Coffee House
Perhaps the city's most popular see-and-be-seen coffee house, with a good-sized patio. ◈ 1105 Denman St • Map G2 • 604 662 3344

8 Wreck Beach
Beneath the cliffs of Point Grey and accessible by steep trails through the rainforest, Wreck Beach is a must for those who enjoy sunbathing *au natural*. Vendors sell everything from piña coladas to tanning oil. ◈ Map A1

9 Delilah's
The West Coast continental menu of this lush and sexy restaurant-bar is bolstered by its martini list, which have many salivating before they even finish reading. ◈ 1789 Comox St • Map H2 • 604 687 3424

10 Odyssey
Though it's been around a long time, this nightclub hasn't lost any of its youthful energy. Each night of the week is different, with drag shows, go-go dancers, male strippers, karaoke, and gay bingo. Odyssey also has what's billed as Vancouver's only private garden bar – secluded, intimate, and one of most popular summer spots for gays and straights alike. ◈ 1251 Howe St • Map J4 • 604 689 5286

While the West End is extremely gay-friendly, care should be taken when visiting Stanley Park at night

Left **Fashions, Robson Street** Right **Italian boots at Bionic Footwear, South Granville**

Top 10 Shopping Destinations

1 Robson Street
Fashionable Robson Street's shopping epicenter is the corner of Burrard and Robson where Virgin Megastore and Roots Canada *(see p72)* make their homes. Browse internationally known clothing, shoe, accessory, and home furnishing stores, or shop for clothing at Canadian-owned Aritzia. Try Lush for bath and body products. Take a breather at any of the many restaurants en route *(see p69)*.

2 Granville Island
There's more to shopping on the Island than just fresh foods at the Public Market: look for silver jewelry and hats among the stalls *(see p80)*. The Net Loft – once used for fishing net repairs – sells neat things, such as handmade paper and hand-dyed clothing. The bountiful Kids Market offers lots of mini-shops and activities for the wee ones *(see pp20–21)*. **Pousse café glassware, Granville Island**

3 Gastown
Gastown's century-old buildings have morphed into one-of-a-kind boutiques, First Nations art galleries, and specialty shops selling everything from buttons to cowboy boots to urban designer clothing. Gastown has long been known for souvenirs, and many retailers selling both classic and kitsch Canadiana line Water Street and the smaller streets leading out from it *(see p61)*.

4 South Granville
South Granville shopping extends along Granville Street from 2nd to 16th avenues. At least a dozen art galleries are found here. The casually elegant strip is home to brand-name and high-end European clothing purveyors such as Bacci, Boboli *(see p81)*, and MaxMara. Fabulous yet affordable footwear awaits at Bionic Footwear and Freedman Shoes. Several lingerie shops, too. ◈ *Map H6*

5 Sinclair Centre
Four heritage buildings are grouped to create an elegant, upscale shopping mall. The three levels of retail indulgence include two floors of exclusive shops offering luxury accessories and clothing from the likes of Versace, Armani, Prada, and DKNY. The lower level has a food fair. ◈ *757 W Hastings* • *Map L3*

6 Chinatown
Vancouver's oldest and largest ethnic shopping area has struggled at times to survive with competition from Richmond's Asian super-malls. Yet Chinatown hangs on, its crowded streets filled with bargain-hunters. Shops selling herbs and potions, exotic delicacies, fresh seafood and vegetables, leather goods, and Asian souvenirs appear elbow to elbow *(see p62)*.

Shopabout Tours, run by knowledgeable locals, hits the city's retail hot spots; call 604 375 1228 or visit www.shopabout.ca

7 Metrotown

Metropolis at Metrotown is BC's largest mall. The atmosphere is charged with the energy of thousands of daily shoppers. Department stores The Bay and Sears (see p112) anchor the mall, with chains and independents well represented by 470 stores. The 17 movie theaters and three games centers ensure that there's entertainment for all, even if shopping's not their thing. ❧ 4720 Kingsway, Burnaby • Map C2 • 604 438 4700

8 Pacific Centre

More than 150 stores and services stretch beneath Granville Street in the heart of downtown Vancouver. After checking out The Bay and Sears (see p112), two major department stores among the many street-level shops, descend to the boutiques and specialty stores below, selling clothing, jewelry, sportswear, gadgets, and more. High-end retailers include Holt Renfrew (see p70).

9 Broadway Avenue

Originally designed to be the city's major thoroughfare, Broadway Avenue's shopping hotspots are located between Main and Alma streets. Mountain Equipment Co-op, at the eastern end, requires a small membership fee, but the sportswear is superb. Going west, the street is dotted with clothing stores, bookshops, and health food stores, particularly at Granville, Arbutus, and Macdonald streets, the latter home to the city's Greektown. ❧ Map A1–B1

Clothing store, Commercial Drive

10 Commercial Drive

The Drive, as it's known locally, is funky and fun, the epitome of hip and casual. Once Vancouver's Little Italy, the area is now an easy-going, multi-ethnic mix of clothing shops, book and magazine stores, vintage-wear boutiques, and second-hand outlets. Start at East Broadway Avenue and Commercial Drive and walk north to Venables Street, admiring the distant Coast Mountains along the way. ❧ Map B2

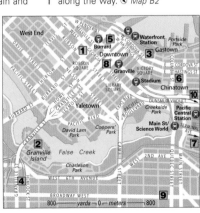

Metropolis at Metrotown has over 4,000 spaces in its free parking lot, or access the mall via SkyTrain, alighting at Metrotown station

55

Left **Vida** Right **A massage at Grotto Spa**

🔟 Spas

1 Willow Stream Spa

The signature treatment, Island Senses for Healthy Energy, includes a pine hydrotherapy bath and restoring massage with aromatic lavender oil. The spa's setting is as romantic as the hotel it's located in. ◉ *Fairmont Empress Hotel, 721 Government St, Victoria • Map P4 • 250 995 4650*

2 Vida

Clients are first analyzed by specialists in Ayurvedic massage for the best way to treat their *dosha*, or body composition, using 5,000-year-old holistic techniques. Then it's on to balancing the *dosha* with dry brushing, a steam in the cedar cabinet, and warm maple-scented oil massages. ◉ *Fairmont Chateau Whistler • Map F1 • 604 938 2086*

Essential oils

3 Spa at the Wedgewood

A full-service hotel spa offering the Chai Soy anti-stress back treatment, which also includes a relaxing scalp and foot massage. The cinnamon enzyme facial, with its skin tightening effect, is a favorite. ◉ *845 Hornby St • Map K3 • 604 689 7777*

4 Grotto Spa

Overlooking an expanse of beach, BC's largest spa resort offers a wide range of treatments, including couple's massages. West Coast seaweed is part of a sensuous scrub, wrap, facial, and massage package. ◉ *Tigh-Na-Mara Seaside Resort and Spa, 1155 Resort Dr, Parksville • Map C4 • 250 248 2072*

5 Absolute Spa at the Century

Escape into relaxation at this gloriously refurbished spa. Choose ancient Moor Mud to whisk away impurities, citrus facial treatments, or a luscious milk bath, just as Cleopatra enjoyed. Chocolate treatments for hands, feet, and body. ◉ *Century Plaza Hotel, 1015 Burrard St • Map J4 • 604 684 2772*

6 La Raffinage Spirit Spa

An oasis offering a holistic approach. Drift through a *reiki* or reflexology session combined with deep-tissue massage. Eye treatments, aromatherapy, and cranial sacral head massages. ◉ *521 W Georgia St • Map K4 • 604 681 9933*

7 silk road spa

This spa takes its cue from the Orient, where tea and relaxation balance each other for harmonious effect. Green tea, an antioxidant, is used in some treatments; aromatherapy enhances others. Products are freshly made. ◉ *1624 Government St, Victoria • Map P1 • 250 704 2688*

BC has the highest standard in Canada for registered massage therapists (RMT); facilities employing RMTs display certification

Spa at Four Seasons Resort Whistler

Top 10 Health and Body Treatments

1 Hot Stone Massage
Locally sourced lava rocks are heated and applied to the body to eliminate stress and restore energy.

2 Seaweed Wraps
West Coast seaweed mud remineralizes the body. Followed by an application of hot towels, a wrap makes for wonderfully soft skin all over.

3 Plant Extracts Facial
Plants such as refreshing cucumber are blended with extracts, including gingko biloba and St. John's Wort, in creams that make the skin glow.

4 Couple's Massage
Sessions for couples focus on full-body relaxation massage with two therapists.

5 Body Sugar Exfoliation
Sugar and essential oils, including Canadian maple, are massaged into the skin to hydrate it and improve circulation.

6 Ayurvedic Steam Cabinet
A steam in a cedar cabinet is an aromatic way to detoxify.

7 Aromatherapy
Aromatic oils are blended for their mental and physical effects, often with a hint of cedar, pine, or lavender.

8 Shower Treatments
Warm water flushed over the body opens blood vessels, rejuvenating the system.

9 Ancient Thai Massage
This massage is done on the floor to combine deep compressions with yoga-like stretches for energy and calm.

10 Chocolate Hand Treatment
Warmed, creamy aromatic chocolate is applied to hands, with silky results.

8 Spa at Four Seasons Resort Whistler
Eucalyptus steam rooms at this sparkling, high-ceilinged spa offer total relaxation. The BC glacial clay wrap uses rockweed and ocean mud. ◈ 4591 Blackcomb Way, Whistler • Map F1 • 604 935 3400

9 skoah
Skin care is the focus at this luxurious spa. Its Facilicious treatment was part of the 2005 Oscar presenters' goody bag. Skin-calming plant extracts are mixed by a staff chemist. ◈ 1011 Hamilton St • Map J5 • 604 642 0200

10 Avello Spa & Health Club
This elegant spa specializes in rock- and hydrotherapy. Water jets eliminate toxins; warm stones create trails of relaxing heat on the body. ◈ Westin Resort, 4090 Whistler Way, Whistler • Map F1 • 604 935 3444

Avello Spa & Health Club

Following pages **Entrance, Marine Heritage Building, Vancouver**

AROUND TOWN

VANCOUVER & VICTORIA'S TOP 10

Left **Waterfront Station** Right **Sidewalk stalls, Chinatown**

Waterfront, Gastown & Chinatown

THE WATERFRONT IS VANCOUVER'S HEART. *After New York, the city is North America's second largest port in both size and tonnage. With the opening of the cruise ship terminal at Canada Place in the mid-1980s, it also became one of the world's major cruise ship ports. A block away, Gastown's origin as a tough mill town is masked by gracefully restored heritage buildings constructed during the boom years of the early 1900s. The Landing, next to Waterfront Station, was one of the first to be renovated. Farther along West Cordova Stree begins Chinatown, the largest in North America after San Francisco's. The area that was once a marsh is now home to over 35,000 people of Chinese descent, though its growth and prosperity did not come easily – it was seen as a threat by seasonal workers, and a closed-door immigration policy was imposed in 1885. Today, Chinatown attracts throngs of shoppers looking for authentic Chinese food and souvenirs.*

Gassy Jack statue, Gastow

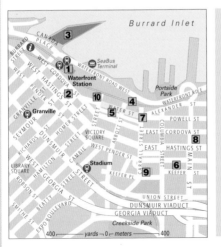

10 Sights

1. Waterfront Station
2. The Lookout!
3. Canada Place
4. Gastown
5. Storyeum
6. Chinatown
7. Maple Tree Square
8. Vancouver Police Centennial Museum
9. Dr. Sun Yat-Sen Classical Chinese Garden
10. Steam Clock

When you buy a ticket to The Lookout! it is valid for the entire day, so you can easily return for a sunset or night view of Vancouver

Five sails, Canada Place

1 Waterfront Station
The station has been a transportation hub since 1887, when the original timber structure welcomed the first cross-Canada passenger train. The present building was built in 1914. With Vancouver Harbour as backdrop, the station's white-columned façade is impressive in a showy way. Inside, murals on the upper walls depict Canadian landscapes. ✪ 601 W Cordova St • Map L3

2 The Lookout!
The showstopper of the Harbour Centre complex is its 581-ft (177-m) tower, home to The Lookout! observation deck. The ride up in the glass-fronted elevator takes a thrilling 50 seconds. From the enclosed viewing deck, the 360-degree view is splendid. On a clear day, you can see Vancouver Island to the west and Washington State's Mount Baker to the south. In the evening, many return to admire the intense sunsets over the water. ✪ 555 W Hastings St • Map L3 • 604 689 0421 • Open May–Oct: 8:30am–10:30pm; Nov–Apr: 9am–9pm • Adm

3 Canada Place
When Canada Place opened in 1986, it was greeted with controversy. Critics commented that its five "sails" were a poor imitation of Australia's Sydney Opera House. The complex is now a key player on the waterfront, which has grown up around it (see pp12–13).

4 Gastown
The cobblestone streets of Gastown have been through many reincarnations. The current one is perhaps the most satisfying. Since the 1970s, the area has worked hard to better itself. The plethora of tawdry souvenir shops have largely been replaced with boutiques selling the work of local designers, a concentration of excellent First Nations and Inuit art galleries, restaurants, and clubs. ✪ Map L3–M3

View of the sunset over Howe Sound, looking toward West Vancouver from The Lookout!

The SkyTrain and SeaBus terminals are located inside Waterfront Station

5 Storyeum

Visitors are treated to a fascinating, fast-paced journey through BC's history – from Native legends to fur trader Hudson's Bay Company's westward drive, to the building of the transnational railway. Actors and technology interact, and audience participation is welcomed as the "citizens" of a Gold Rush town bring history alive through dance and song *(see pp16–17)*.

6 Chinatown

Stretching from Gore Avenue west to Carrall Street between Pender and Keefer streets, Chinatown dates back to the 1880s and the building of the Canadian Pacific Railway, when as many as 20,000 Chinese came to Canada. Today it is North America's second-largest Chinatown. Shops with their vegetable stalls spill onto the sidewalks. The Millennium Gate straddles Pender near Taylor Street and is the best place to start a walking tour of this lively area. ◈ *Map L4–M4*

Triangular Building, at Maple Tree Square

7 Maple Tree Square

The city of Vancouver has its roots in this small square. Standing atop his barrel of beer, the statue of John "Gassy Jack" Deighton commemorates Gastown's founder. The talkative publican built the city's first saloon with the help of thirsty sawmill workers. A maple tree here was once a popular meeting place until it was destroyed in the Great Fire of 1886. Gaoler's Mews was the site of the city's first prison, as well as the home of the city's first policeman, Constable Jonathan Miller. ◈ *Water St at Carrall St • Map M3*

Chinatown lamppost

8 Vancouver Police Centennial Museum

Enter the old city morgue, now the police museum's forensic laboratory, and it's not difficult to imagine the coroner leaning over the slab, about to start an examination. Housed in the former Coroner Court, built in 1932, the museum has fine exhibits of counterfeit money, antique firearms, and street weaponry. Always popular is the knife room. Unsolved murders are depicted in displays complete with dummies and period costumes. ◈ *240 E Cordova St • Map M4 • 604 665 3346 • Adm*

An Iron Road, Coast to Coast

The grand saga of Canadian railways is a tale of power and pain. In 1886, Prime Minister John A. Macdonald fulfilled his promise to build a cross-Canada railway to unite the new Dominion of Canada. The first transcontinental passenger train arrived in Vancouver on May 23, 1887, where Waterfront Station now stands. The whole city came out to celebrate. Even the ships in the harbor were decked out in flags. The "Iron Road" was completed at last. Sadly, progress came at the loss of many lives, including more than 600 Chinese laborers.

Dr. Sun Yat-Sen Classical Chinese Garden

his Ming Dynasty-style garden, the 'st built outside China, opened in 986. It re-creates the private 'eas typically found in a Ming cholar's home. With its mean-ering paths, corridors and court-ards, and asymmetrically placed cks, the garden invites contem-ation on the beauty and rhythm f nature. Plants include local nd traditional Chinese varieties, ich as flowering gingko trees nd twisted pines. ◈ *578 Carrall St* Map M4 • *604 662 3207* • Adm

Steam Clock

Said to be the world's first eam-operated clock, this land-ark is one of the most photo-aphed in the city. But it's not antique. Local horologist Ray-ond Saunders based the 16-ft-(-m-) tall clock, at the corner of 'ater and Cambie streets, on an 375 model. Be patient, and wait r the explosion of steam every minutes. Erected in 1977, the onze and gold clock strikes 'estminster chimes every hour the hour. ◈ *Water St at Cambie* • Map L3

am clock, Gastown

A Day in Waterfront, Gastown & Chinatown

Morning

Begin at **Canada Place** *(see pp12–13)* for a view of the harbor. After strolling the promenade for 20 minutes, walk east to **Waterfront Station**, 601 W Cordova St, peeking at the scenic murals inside. At the junc-tion of Cordova and Water streets, continue two blocks along Water to Cambie St to admire Gas-town's **steam clock**.

A block further is **Storyeum** *(see pp16–17)*. Enjoy the 72-minute historical pageant before walking the block back to **Water Street Café** *(see p65)* for lunch.

Afternoon

Walk east 10 minutes to **Maple Tree Square**, at Water and Carrall sts, to see the statue of "Gassy Jack" Deighton, proprietor of the city's first saloon.

Walk four blocks south on Cambie St to W Pender and the **Dr. Sun Yat-Sen Classical Chinese Garden**. Explore the peaceful spot for 30 minutes, then spend another half hour at the adjoining **Chinese Cultural Centre Museum and Archives**, viewing exhibits on history, arts, and culture.

Head east on Pender St, admiring **Millennium Gate** as you walk through it into **Chinatown**. Spend the afternoon exploring the multitude of shops, keeping an eye on the wooden her-itage buildings you pass.

End the day feasting on Cantonese dishes at **Floata Seafood** *(see p65)*. If the Chinatown Night Market is on (6:30pm–11pm Fri–Sun), add on a market stroll.

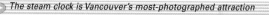

Left **The Irish Heather** Right **Herons Lounge**

TOP 10 Bars & Clubs

1 The Irish Heather
There are about 100 single malts and Irish whiskeys to choose from in this attractive pub. Try the food, too – the menu includes many tasty pub favorites such as bangers 'n mash. ⚅ 217 Carrall St • Map M4 • 604 688 9779

2 Rossinis
A cozy spot to hear live jazz, offered nightly, while enjoying Italian fare. Children welcome. ⚅ 162 Water St • Map L3 • 604 408 1300

3 The Brickyard Bar
Local and touring bands play a wide range of music here, appreciated by a casual 20-something crowd. ⚅ 315 Carrall St • Map M4 • 604 685 3922

4 Cascades Lounge
Sip a lunchtime cocktail with pasta buffet or slip from happy hours to jazz-fuelled evenings with a pianist or jazz diva. The dining menu features light, exquisite dishes. Patio in summer. ⚅ Pan Pacific Hotel, 300-999 Canada Place Way • Map L2 • 604 895 2480

5 Steamworks Brewing
Complement your pizza, pasta, burger, or satay with one of the several delicious beers brewed here, such as pale ale, nutbrown, or stout. ⚅ 375 Water St • Map L3 • 604 689 2739

6 Lamplighter
This historic pub opened in 1899. A laid-back crowd relaxes over drinks such as Guinness on tap and shooters. DJs and local and imported bands play indie, jazz or hip-hop. ⚅ 210 Abbott St • Map L3 • 604 681 6666

7 Shine NightClub
Dance to DJ-driven music, including rock, rap, electro, dancehall and reggae. Thursday night is classic 1980s tunes. ⚅ 364 Water St • Map L3 • 604 408 4321

8 Alibi Room
DJs play funk, soul and hip-hop in this warm two-level space. Catch art shows and movie screenings in the lower lounge. A great place to meet people. ⚅ 1 Alexander St • Map M3 • 604 623 33..

9 Herons Lounge
With its array of trees and plants, this luxurious lounge has an outdoor ambience. Sink into an upholstered armchair and enjoy a chilled martini. ⚅ Fairmont Waterfront Hotel, 900 Canada Place • Map K3 • 604 691 1818

10 Sonar
The high-energy crowd pulses to underground sou.. There are four ba.. and plenty of dim lit corners to explo.. Occasional live ac.. ⚅ 66 Water St • Ma.. L3 • 604 683 6695

Note: Unless otherwise stated, all bars, clubs, and restaurants accept credit cards

Price Categories

For a three-course meal for one with half a bottle of wine (or equivalent meal), taxes, and extra charges.

$	under $20
$$	$20–$35
$$$	$35–$60
$$$$	$60–$85
$$$$$	over $85

above **Water Street Café**

🔟 Restaurants & Cafés

1 Imperial Chinese Seafood Restaurant

This restaurant, serving superb Cantonese food, is located in the 1929 Art Deco Marine Building. ◈ 355 Burrard St • Map K3 • 604 688 8191 • $$$$

2 Aqua Riva

Overlooking the harbor, the mood here is low-key chic. Local produce, West Coast-inspired cioppino, and wood-oven pizza are featured. ◈ 200 Granville St • Map L3 • 604 683 5599 • $$$

3 Sitar Restaurant

Classic North Indian dishes such as mouth-watering butter chicken are served in a soothing setting. Many vegetarian choices. Licensed. ◈ 8 Powell St • Map M3 • 604 687 0049 • $$$

4 Buddhist Vegetarian Restaurant

There's nothing fancy about this restaurant, but the choice of 200 vegan dishes is impressive. No MSG, artificial flavor, preservatives, or honey used. ◈ 137 E Pender St • Map M4 • 604 683 8816 • $

5 Momo Sushi

Fresh sushi is the featured attraction, with teriyaki, tempura and sashimi also available. Expect lineups at lunch. ◈ 6-375 Water St • Map L3 • 604 683 7632 • $$

6 Wild Rice

Upbeat house music beckons you to try spicy, modern Chinese cuisine in this cozy space. Small but good wine list. ◈ 117 W Pender St • Map L4 • 604 642 2882 • no reservations accepted • $$

7 Al Porto Ristorante

Pastas, fish, meat, and pizza are the highlights at this bright, lively Italian trattoria. More than 200 wines on offer, 80 from BC. ◈ 321 Water St • Map L3 • 604 683 8376 • $$$

8 Water Street Café

Continental food made with fresh seafood and local ingredients is the draw here. Local beers on draft and a fine selection of BC wines. Lovely patio in summer. ◈ 300 Water St • Map L3 • 604 689 2832 • $$$

9 Brioche Urban Baking

Diners cram into this 30-seat café, enjoying the casually trendy ambience and the rustic Italian meals. Take out available. ◈ 401 W Cordova St • Map L3 • 604 682 4037 • not licensed • $

🔟 Floata Seafood Restaurant

Delectable dim sum dishes arrive in a flurry of carts. There's also a Cantonese-style menu. ◈ 180 Keefer St • Map M4 • 604 602 0368 • $$$

Following pages **Downtown Vancouver by night**

Left **Shoppers, Robson Street** Right **Cyclists, False Creek Seawalk**

Downtown

_V_ANCOUVER'S DOWNTOWN CORE _is a blend of old and new, all nicely contained in a walkable package that extends from BC Place Stadium to the West End. The city's first church sits at the corner of_
Georgia and Burrard streets, hemmed in by glass-walled office towers. The landmark Fairmont Hotel Vancouver graces the opposite corner, a glorious reminder of yesteryear. Alive with activity, downtown hums all day and much of the night. The core includes high-density residential areas, street and mall shopping, theaters, music venues, restaurants, and nightclubs, all adding up to a pleasant, invigorating energy._

Stained glass, Christ Church Cathedral

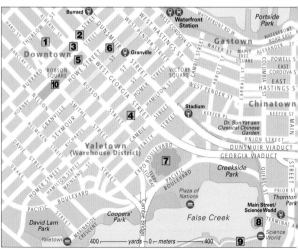

1 Robson Street

West End residents, the city's urban chic, international celebrities, and tourists alike flock to Robson Street to join the bustle of shoppers. Part of the fun is people watching over a specialty coffee, then browsing the brand name and independent Canadian and international shops. Slip down a side street to get a taste of the historic West End, Canada's most densely populated area. ✆ *Map H2–K4*

2 Christ Church Cathedral

A gem in the heart of the city and once a beacon for mariners entering Vancouver's harbor, Christ Church Cathedral, consecrated in 1895, was designed in the Gothic Revival style. The interior has impressive old-growth Douglas fir ceiling beams. Three of the 32 stained-glass windows are by the British artist William Morris; look for them in the office vestibule. In 2004, as part of a major renovation, a brand new Kenneth Jones organ was installed. ✆ *690 Burrard St • Map K3 • 604 682 3848*

Fairmont Hotel Vancouver

3 Fairmont Hotel Vancouver

Begun in 1928 by the Canadian Pacific Railway, construction on the city's most famous hotel halted with the 1929 stock market crash. Its steel skeleton sat until 1939, when it was hastily finished for the visit of King George VI. Features include a steep copper roof with impish gargoyles. Stroll through the lobby or enjoy a drink in the lounge, all the while admiring the lavishness. ✆ *900 W Georgia St • Map K3 • 604 684 3131*

4 Library Square

The new Vancouver Central Library, designed in part by renowned architect Moshe Safdie, opened in 1995. At first critized by some for its resemblance to a Roman coliseum, it soon became universally popular. Library Square takes up a whole city block, and includes the library; a seven-story, glass-roofed promenade; the Federal Tower, housing government offices; souvenir shops, a coffee bar, and take-out restaurants. The promenade is an ideal place to relax and people watch. ✆ *Corner of Robson & Homer sts • Map K4*

Vancouver Public Library, Library Square

Fountains at the Vancouver Art Gallery

Vancouver Art Gallery
When the Court House was erected in 1912, designed by Francis Rattenbury, one of BC's flashiest architects, its solid form symbolized the British Empire at its peak. Another controversial architect, Arthur Erickson, supervised the redesign of the building when it became the Vancouver Art Gallery in the mid-1980s. Inside, the Emily Carr collection is Canada's largest. Contemporary photoconceptual work also has a prominent place *(see pp18–19)*.

Pacific Centre
Quality department stores The Bay and Sears anchor the host of smaller shops in this huge mall, which incorporates cascading fountains and a three-story waterfall. Restaurants and takeaways dot the concourse. *◈ 609 Granville St with entrances via Robson, Dunsmuir & W Georgia sts • Map K3 • 604 688 7235 • Open 10am–7pm Mon–Wed, 10am–9pm Thu–Fri, 9:30am–6pm Sat, 11am–6pm Sun*

BC Sports Hall of Fame and Museum
Twenty galleries showcase BC's sports history from the 1860s onward in a 20,000 sq ft (1,858 sq m) space located in BC Place Stadium *(see p42)*. Interactive displays provide fascinating details of the lives of famous athletes such as skier Nancy Green and sprinter Harry Jerome. The Participation Gallery is especially fun for kids. *◈ 777 Pacific Blvd S, Gate A • Map L4 • 604 687 5520 • Adm*

Science World
The striking geodesic dome housing Science World's many interactive galleries and travelling exhibitions was built for Expo '86. Visitors can play with magnetic liquids, touch animal skin and bones, and check out exhibits on motion, and energy, as well as laser shows. The Alcan OMNIMAX Theatre's giant screen fits into the dome's curves *(see pp22–3)*.

Terry Fox's Marathon of Hope

Born in Winnipeg in 1958, Terry Fox grew up in a Vancouver suburb. When just 18 years old, he was diagnosed with bone cancer and had his leg amputated. Three years later, in 1980, Terry dipped his artificial leg into the Atlantic Ocean, beginning his Marathon of Hope across Canada to raise money for cancer research. After 143 days and 3,339 mi (5,373 km), Terry stopped his run. Cancer had spread to his lungs. He died in 1981, shortly after realizing his dream of raising $1 for every Canadian – over $24 million. Annual Terry Fox runs worldwide continue Terry's mission.

Interactive display, Science World

9 False Creek Seawalk

False Creek (see p79) once covered an extensive part of the downtown area. It now ends at Quebec Street, site of Science World. The paved False Creek Seawalk joins English Bay Seawalk just east of Burrard Bridge and circles the creek. It's ideal for in-line skaters, cyclists, and walkers. Access to False Creek ferries is available at several points along the seawalk.  ✆ Map H6–M5

Plexiglass dome, Robson Square

10 Robson Square and Law Courts

Spanning several blocks, the four-level Robson Square was designed by BC architect Arthur Erickson. On the south side of Robson Street, a cascading waterfall and trees cool the steps near *Spring*, a red steel sculpture by Alan Chung Hung. On the level above, inside the Law Courts, is a pond with seating and a good view. Jack Harman's sculpture, *Themis Goddess of Justice*, presides over the Great Hall, with its expanses of glass. ✆ *800 block Robson St • Map J4 • 604 660 8989*

A Downtown Walk

Morning

Start at **BC Place Stadium** *(see p42)*, exploring the **BC Sports Hall of Fame and Museum** for about an hour. Exiting the museum, head west toward Robson St, passing by the **Terry Fox Memorial**, a tribute to the local hero who raised millions of dollars for cancer research.

Continue west three blocks along Robson St to Homer St, and **Library Square** *(see p69)*. Drop in to have a look at the building's airy promenade before walking west on Robson St to **Pacific Centre**. Peruse the shops for about an hour, then exit the mall and cross Howe St to the **Vancouver Art Gallery**. Enjoy a salad and sandwich in its casually elegant **Gallery Café**, snagging a patio table if weather permits.

Afternoon

After lunch, head to the fourth floor of the **Vancouver Art Gallery** *(see pp18–19)* and the wonderful **Emily Carr Collection**. Begin by watching the 15-minute video about this remarkable painter of forests and totem poles.

Exiting the gallery, cross Robson St and stroll through lovely **Robson Square**. Then it's on to shopping along **Robson Street** *(see p69)*. Satisfy a sweet tooth at one of the several chocolate shops. Loop back to Burrard St.

End the day with a treat at **Kamei Royale Japanese Restaurant** *(see p73)*, at 1030 W Georgia St. The excellent sushi chefs welcome you enthusiastically.

Left **lululemon atheltica** Right **Smoked salmon gift boxes, Salmon Village**

TOP 10 Shopping

1 Roots Canada
Classic Canadian-designed sportswear and leatherwear. Outfitter to the 2004 Candian, US, and British Summer Olympic teams. ✆ *1001 Robson St • Map J3 • 604 683 4305*

2 lululemon athletica
This Vancouver-based company sells wildly popular men's and women's yoga apparel, athletic gear, and casual wear. ✆ *1148 Robson St • Map J3 • 604 681 3118*

3 Alberni Street Liquor Store
This BC Liquor Store carries a large variety of wines, spirits, and beers, as well as an excellent array of sought-after BC ice wine, made from frozen grapes. ✆ *1120 Alberni St • Map J3 • 604 660 4572*

4 Rendezvous Art Gallery
Contemporary and traditional Canadian paintings and sculptures reflect West Coast beauty. First Nations and Inuit artists are well represented. ✆ *671 Howe St • Map K3 • 604 687 7466*

5 Daniel Le Chocolat Belge
Belgian chocolate and all-natural or organic ingredients are used to create the delicious pralines and champagne, coffee, and lemon truffles sold here. ✆ *1105 Robson St • Map J3 • 604 688 9624*

6 Grand Maple Gifts
Great Canadian souvenirs, from quality T-shirts, BC jade jewelry, and First Nations crafts to maple syrup products and ice-wine chocolates. ✆ *1046 Robson St • Map J3 • 604 681 8979*

7 Salmon Village
This long-established local company sells top-quality wild and farmed BC salmon. ✆ *779 Thurlow St • Map J3 • 604 685 3378*

8 John Fluevog Boots & Shoes Ltd
Fluevog's funky and trendy, yet sturdy, shoes and boots are snapped up by the fashion savvy. ✆ *837 Granville St • Map K4 • 604 688 2828*

9 Jones the Jeweler
Artfully set diamonds mined in Canada and beautifully-crafted-gold creations make perfect gifts. ✆ *807 Hornby St • Map J3 • 604 681 9548*

10 Escents Aromatherapy
Treat yourself to fine aroma-therapy bath and body products made by this local company from pure plant essences and essential oils. ✆ *1172 Robson St • Map J3 • 604 682 0041*

Price Categories

For a three-course meal for one with half a bottle of wine (or equivalent meal), taxes, and extra charges.

$	under $20
$$	$20–$35
$$$	$35–$60
$$$$	$60–$85
$$$$$	over $85

above **Don Francesco**

🔟 Restaurants

1 Kamei Royale Japanese Restaurant
Delight in traditional grilled dishes, or in the house-original rolls at the sushi bar. ◈ *1030 W Georgia St • Map K3 • 604 687 8588 • $$$*

2 Bacchus Restaurant
Dine in style on outstanding food served in a formal setting. Brunch, lunch, and afternoon tea served, too. ◈ *Wedgewood Hotel, 845 Hornby St • Map J4 • 604 608 5319 • $$$$$*

3 Aria Restaurant & Lounge
Relish dishes such as wild salmon and caribou accompanied by fine wines in this contemporary restaurant. ◈ *Westin Grand Vancouver Hotel, 433 Robson St • Map K4 • 604 647 2521 • $$$$*

4 CinCin Ristorante & Bar
Delicious wood-oven pizza, pasta, and risotto are served in this large Mediterranean-themed restaurant popular with visiting Hollywood stars. ◈ *1154 Robson St • Map J3 • 604 688 7338 • $$$$*

5 Diva at the Met
In the open kitchen, chefs prepare dishes featuring West Coast ingredients. The exceptional wine list is topped with BC wines. ◈ *Metropolitan Hotel, 645 Howe St • Map K3 • 604 602 7788 • $$$$*

6 Salathai Thai Restaurant
Enjoy tasty Thai food prepared with homemade sauces, served in a tropical setting. Friendly, attentive service. ◈ *102-888 Burrard St • Map J3 • 604 683 7999 • $$*

7 Don Francesco
Step into Tuscany and choose from a large selection of game, seafood, beef, fowl, and pasta dishes. ◈ *860 Burrard St • Map J3 • 604 685 7770 • $$$$*

8 Raincity Grill
Pacific waters lap outside this trend-setting English Bay restaurant; sunsets are a bonus. The focus is on regional, seasonal, and organic food. ◈ *1193 Denman St • Map G3 • 604 685 7337 • $$$$*

9 Le Crocodile
Pan-seared *foie gras* is the signature dish at this elegant French restaurant. French wines are highlighted. ◈ *100-909 Burrard St • Map J3 • 604 669 4298 • $$$*

🔟 El Patio
The homemade sangria goes exceptionally well with the several tapas on offer. Or sample the elaborate *paella Valenciana*. Lovely rooftop patio. ◈ *891 Cambie St • Map K4 • 604 681 9149 • $$*

Left **Crush Champagne Lounge** Right **The New Yuk Yuk's**

🔟 Bars and Clubs

1 La Bodega Restaurante & Tapa-Bar
Enter and you may think you've been whisked off to Spain. Pitchers of sangria often dot the tables, but wine and beers are also perfectly suited to the tapas. ✎ 1277 Howe St • Map J4 • 604 684 8815

2 Commodore Ballroom
A Vancouver institution since 1929, the club hosts ticketed rock, pop, blues, and jazz acts. Tuesday is disco night.
✎ 868 Granville St • Map K4 • 604 739 4550 • www.hob.com/venues/concerts/commodore

3 The New Yuk Yuk's
International stand-up comedy, with a great sound system. Tuesday's Crash and Burn show features five new comics and a guest headliner. ✎ 1015 Burrard St • Map J4 • 604 696 9857

4 Caprice Nightclub
Upscale club with two levels and a huge dance floor. Top 40 and retro nights. ✎ 967 Granville St • Map K4 • 604 681 2114

5 Railway Club
Live country, folk, roots, and funk at this legendary club. Microbrews, quality wines, and scotch and martini lists. ✎ 579 Dunsmuir St • Map K3 • 604 681 1625

6 ginger 62
Live and spun house, reggae, R&B, and soul at this retro-style lounge. Tasty snacks forestall the effects of specialty martinis and cocktails. ✎ 1219 Granville St • Map J4 • 604 688 5494

7 Crush Champagne Lounge
A small dance floor enhances the intimate feel. Let the sommelier suggest a wine, or opt for a champagne cocktail. ✎ 1180 Granville St • Map J4 • 604 684 0355

8 AuBAR Nightclub
Top 40 selections reverberate off the lofty ceiling while candlelit tables inspire romantic whisperings. Dress to impress. ✎ 674 Seymour St • Map K3 • 604 648 2227

9 O'Doul's Restaurant & Bar
Live jazz nightly in an Old World room of reds and golds. Detailed cocktail list, bolstered by scotch, whiskey, beers, and a full wine list. ✎ 1300 Robson St • Map J3 • 604 661 1400

10 SkyBar
Kick off with martinis, then dinner, before dancing the night away. Four bars, rooftop patio, themed evenings. ✎ 670 Smithe • Map K4 • 604 697 9199

Call ahead to check opening hours, as times may vary according to the day of the week. Some nightclubs are closed Sundays

Price Categories

For a three-course meal for one with half a bottle of wine (or equivalent meal), taxes, and extra charges.

$	under $20
$$	$20–$35
$$$	$35–$60
$$$$	$60–$85
$$$$$	over $85

above **Café S'il Vous Plait**

10 Cheap Eats

1 Café S'il Vous Plait
Macaroni and cheese, chili, and other comfort foods are served in this quirky café, along with Japanese *udon*. Freshly baked pies and avocado-banana shakes are a treat. ◈ 500 Robson St • Map K4 • 604 688 7216 • $

2 Egoziku Noodle Café
Great big bowls of warming *ramen* soup. Choose from a miso, soy, or salt base. ◈ 270 Robson St • Map K4 • 604 685 9466 • $

3 Library Square
Find a table and energize with a slice of Flying Wedge pizza, or choose between a Blenz coffee with a Rocky Road square and a Bogen Früz yogurt cone. ◈ 345 Robson St • Map K4 • $

4 Kichi Sushi
Well-placed booths in a spacious room. Daily sushi or teriyaki specials are always fresh. Or ask about the "super ideal items." ◈ 778 Robson St • Map K4 • 604 669 3998 • $

5 Bellaggio Café
Snag a booth in this stylish Italian restaurant, and be sure to ask about the daily pasta special, served with garlic bread. BC wines featured. ◈ 773 Hornby St • Map K3 • 604 408 1281 • $

6 Pacific Centre Food Fair
Choose from Japanese or Chinese made-to-order dishes, pizza, burgers, tacos, juices, and frozen yogurts. ◈ Granville & Dunsmuir sts entrance • Map K3 • 604 688 7235 • $

7 Culinaria
Indulge in a three-course gourmet meal, whipped up by students of Dubrulle Culinary Arts, that's easy on the pocketbook. ◈ 609 Granville St • Map K3 • 604 639 2055 • $$

8 Pita Wrap
Middle Eastern-style meat or vegetarian combos and hearty falafel wraps at this tiny takeout joint require two hands to hold. ◈ 708 Robson St • Map K3 • $

9 Salad Maison
A simple Korean café with a 40-item salad bar. Fast and filling spicy squid rice, Korean barbecue, and soups. ◈ 345 Robson St • Map K4 • $$

10 La Vieille France
Crepes are the specialty at this utilitarian spot. The berry and cream cheese, and spinach and feta are favorites. ◈ 380 Robson St • Map K4 • 604 689 9885 • $

Note: Not all restaurants in Vancouver are licensed; phone ahead to inquire

Left *Gate to the Pacific Northwest,* Vanier Park Right **Boy mummy,** Vancouver Museum

South Granville & Yaletown

THE NEIGHBORHOODS OF SOUTH GRANVILLE AND YALETOWN *are separated by a drive across Granville Bridge or a ferry ride across False Creek.* On the south shore, South Granville offers a pleasant mix of upscale shops and restaurants. Granville Island is a bustling labyrinth of converted warehouses overlooking False Creek. The centerpiece is the large public market. Yaletown, on the north shore of the creek, began life as a railway works yard. Since the early 1990s, Yaletown has undergone a furiously fast transformation. The once-decrepit area now booms with offices, condos, boutiques, nightclubs, brew pubs, and restaurants.

RCMP schooner, Vancouver Maritime Museum

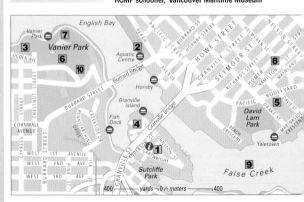

→ *A slew of commercial art galleries have earned South Granville Street between 5th and 15th avenues the nickname Gallery Row*

ew of West End high-rises from Granville Island

1 Granville Island

The original mud flats of False eek were a fishing ground for e Squamish people. Industry oved in, polluting much of the rn-of-the-19th-century city. In e 1970s, all that changed with e redevelopment of Granville land. Under the aegis of the deral government, heavy indus-y moved out and Granville and quickly became a colorful, stling community. Free street rking is available with a three-ur limit, or choose paid parking covered lots *(see pp20–21).*

2 Sunset Beach

The white sands of Sunset each, which marks the end of e English Bay seawall and the art of False Creek, provide an eal setting for relaxing, tan-ng, or swimming. Summertime ater temperatures rise to 65°F 8°C), and lifeguards are on duty om mid-May to Labour Day. The estern end of Sunset Beach ovides a good view of the gray anite *Inukshuk (see p36)*. The ncouver Aquatic Centre, at the st end of the beach, has an ympic-size swimming and ving pools, a sauna, a whirlpool, d a steam room. False Creek rries *(see p21)* dock behind e center. ◈ *Map G3–H4*

3 Vancouver Maritime Museum

Highlights of the West Coast's rich maritime history include sea-going canoes and a 1928 RCMP schooner. Kids can play with the discovery center's telescopes, computer games, and underwater robot *(see p34).* ◈ *1905 Ogden Ave • Map G4 • 604 257 8300 • Open Sep–May: 10am–5pm Tue–Sat, noon–5pm Sun; May–Sep: 10am–5pm daily • Adm*

4 Granville Island Museums

The fine collections of this three-in-one museum focus on fishing, trains, and sea vessels *(see p35).* Exhibits include 500 hand-tied fishing flies. ◈ *1502 Duranleau St • Map H5 • 604 683 1939 • Open 10am–5:30pm Tue–Sun • Adm*

View of Sunset Beach

5 Roundhouse Arts & Recreation Centre

Located on Beach Avenue in a former Canadian Pacific Railway switching building, the Roundhouse includes theater and gallery spaces and a host of community arts and athletic programs. It also houses the locomotive that pulled the first passenger train to Vancouver in 1887 in a splendid glassed-in space.
🚇 181 Roundhouse Mews
• Map K5 • 604 713 1800

Plaque, Roundhouse

6 H.R. MacMillan Space Centre

Space lore is presented in child-friendly, hands-on displays and multimedia shows at the space center. A demonstration theater, the Virtual Voyages' full-motion simulator, and the Cosmic Courtyard's interactive gallery bring space to life. The Planetarium's multimedia shows feature space and astronomy inside a 65-ft (20-m) dome, and its laser shows set to music are always popular. 🚇 1100 Chestnut St
• Map G4 • 604 738 7827 • Adm

7 Vanier Park

Vanier Park is a calming oasis in the midst of the city. Boats sail by on English Bay, kites fly overhead, and pedestrians and cyclists pass through on their way to Kitsilano Beach or Granville Island. Coast Salish people once inhabited the park area. It is now home to the H.R. MacMillan Space Centre, Vancouver Museum, and Vancouver Maritime Museum (see p77). 🚇 Map G4

8 Yaletown Warehouse District

Warehouses have been transformed into lofts and stores, café terraces have sprung up on old loading docks, and high-rises have filled Yaletown's skyline. Along with the new residents has come a facelift. Homer, Hamilton, and Mainland streets have been spruced up, making the most of heritage architectural features, including red brick and arched doorways. Numerous brew pubs and nightclubs keep the area hopping at night. 🚇 Map J4–K5

Yaletown's Railway History

Yaletown was first settled by Canadian Pacific Railway (CPR) train crews and laborers who arrived after the CPR closed its construction camp in Yale, BC, on completion of the transcontinental railway to Vancouver in 1887. In the early 1990s, Yaletown was still the decaying heart of the city's remaining industrial activity, when a development plan jump-started its transformation into a lively urban area. In just over a decade, Yaletown has become Vancouver's hottest community.

Renovated warehouses, Yaletown

Boats moored on False Creek, south side

9 False Creek

As its name implies, False Creek is not a creek at all but a saltwater inlet. In the heart of the city, it extends east from Burrard Bridge to Science World (see pp22–3). In the 1850s, Captain G.H. Richards sailed up this body of water, which then covered what is now Chinatown, eastward to Clark Drive, hoping to find the Fraser River. Disappointed, he named it False Creek. The mud flats Richards saw served as fishing grounds for the Squamish people. Sawmills later set up on the south shore, railyards on the north. Today, paved paths flank both sides (see p71), and boats and small ferries (see p21) ply the waters. ◈ Map J6–L5

10 Vancouver Museum

Canada's largest civic museum boasts re-creations of Vancouver's history, including an immigrant ship and a fur-trading post. Artifacts from a huge collection, much of which was donated by locals, make up natural history, archaeology, Asian arts, and ethnology exhibits. The Egyptian boy mummy is one of the museum's biggest attractions. ◈ 1100 Chestnut • Map G5 • 604 736 4431 • Open am–5pm Tue–Sun, Thu to 9pm • Adm

A Day in Yaletown & at Granville Island

Morning

Start in **Yaletown** at the corner of Drake and Hamilton streets for a 15-minute stroll north on Hamilton, noting its historic buildings. At Helmcken St, turn right, then right again at Mainland St. Spend half an hour in the shops, ending at **Obsessions** (see p81).

Cross Pacific Blvd to admire the **Roundhouse**'s Steam Train 374. Take 15 minutes exploring the complex, then hop on the **Aquabus** (see p21) from the dock behind the center for the short trip to Granville Island (see pp20–21). For a fun hour, wander the public market, buying food for a casual lunch on a waterside bench, or at a table inside.

Afternoon

Exit the market's east side. Continue on Johnston St past **Ocean Cement**, the island's last industry. Turn right on Old Bridge St to watch the glass blower at **New-Small and Sterling Glass Studio** (see p20). Walk to **Railspur Alley**, on your left. Browse the shops for 20 minutes, then cross adjacent Railspur Park to Cartwright St. Turn left and walk to the end, to **The Mound**. The view is worth the 20-minute climb.

Back on Johnston St, head west to peek at the modern art in the **Charles H. Scott Gallery** (see p35). Take Anderson St to Duranleau, and the **Granville Island Museums** (see p35), allowing yourself an hour there.

End the day at **Bridges** (1696 Duranleau St), choosing between its fine dining room and casual bistro.

For a pleasant under-one-hour trip round False Creek, catch a mini-ferry from one of the Granville Island docks See pp20–21

79

Left **Fresh striped pasta, specialty food stall** Right **Hat display, craft stall**

Top 10 Granville Island Public Market

1 Public Market Building
At Granville Island's west end is the large public market, housed in part in a wood-frame, corrugated tin-clad warehouse. Built in the early 1920s by the Island's first tenant, BC Equipment, this structure set the architectural style of the Island. The timbered beams and massive pulleys and hooks once pulled rope coils from one area to the other. *See pp20–21.*

2 Food Courts
Two food courts offer sit-down and takeaway food, including Greek, Mexican, Thai, Chinese, and Canadian. Patience and strategy may be required to land one of the limited indoor tables.

3 Local Produce and Seafood
Artful displays tempt with fruits and vegetables – much of it organic – fresh from the orchards and farms of BC. Okanagan cherries, apples, and peaches are a summer delight. BC wild salmon is another market specialty – both fresh and smoked in gift boxes.

4 Olde World Fudge
Irresistible Belgian chocolate treats are concocted on-site in a copper vat. Assorted gift boxes include fudge, toffee, brittles, and caramel apples. Samples available!

5 Stuart's Bakery
Mouth-watering pies, chocolate confections, and pastries fill one counter; multigrain, cheese, and other loaves crowd the other.

6 Eating Outdoors
Enjoy your takeaway food o just relax at the rustic seating areas overlooking False Creek. Exit the west side of the marke for views of the marina. On the east side, enjoy free entertain-ment in the Market Courtyard. The courtyard's worn floor plan from its days as an industrial dock add to the charm.

7 Craft and Specialty Stall
Day vendors sell an assort-ment of locally made wares, including seasonal and specialt items. Bowls made of BC woo Thai curry sauces, herb seed-lings, homemade pies, and jew elry are just the start. Vendors may not be located in the same place from day to day.

8 Buskers
Licensed musicians, magi-cians, clowns, jugglers, and other talented folk entertain fre of charge, though a donation is always appreciated.

9 Flower Shops
Abundance and quality are the themes at the market's flow shops. It is worth a stop just to admire the gorgeous blooms a take in the heady scents.

10 Marina
At the marina on the mar-ket's west side you'll find fancy yachts, simple sail boats, and t occasional fishing boat. Tall shi dock here during festivals.

Left **Sleek housewares, Roost Homeware**   Right **The latest fashions, Boboli**

TOP10 Shopping

1 Urban Fare
This grocery, open daily from 6am to midnight, offers staples along with its organic and specialty products. Cooking classes are held several nights a week. ✆ *177 Davie St • Map K5 • 604 975 7550*

2 Obsessions
A fascinating array of personal and household designer items, all with modern twists. Jewelry made from sterling silver and precious stones. ✆ *289 Davie St • Map K5 • 604 683 0188*

3 Bernstein & Gold
Carry or ship home Egyptian cotton linens, Italian bedding, tapestries, and leather journals, picnic baskets, cashmere throws, and Fortuni lamps. ✆ *1168 Hamilton St • Map K5 • 604 687 1535*

4 Roost Homeware
Wonderful selection of housewares, some imports – such as luxurious Australian mohair blankets – and some by local talents on the rise. ✆ *1192 Hamilton St • Map K5 • 604 708 0084*

5 Circle Craft Co-op
The best of BC crafts, from handmade clothing to one-of-a-kind jewelry to wall art, ceramics, and hand-blown glass. ✆ *1666 Johnston St • Map H5 • 604 669 8021*

6 Vansanji Boutique
The latest in trend-setting brand-name clothes for men and women arrive regularly from around the world. Local designers, such as Jason Matlo, are featured, too. Great shoe selection. ✆ *1012 Mainland St • Map K5 • 604 669 0882*

7 Forge and Form
High-end gold and silver jewelry with precious stones. Bold rings, fluid necklaces. ✆ *1334 Cartwright St • Map H5 • 604 684 6298*

8 Beadworks
Over 30,000 jewelry beads and related books make the choice fascinating and fun. Make your own earrings on site. ✆ *1666 Johnston St • Map H5 • 604 682 2323*

9 Malaspina Printmakers Gallery
Prints by Canadian (particularly BC) and international artists with images and styles – from photorealism to abstract – to suit all tastes. ✆ *1555 Duranleau St • Map H5 • 604 688 1724*

10 Boboli
Trend-setting styles from a variety of men's and women's lines, including Missoni, Issey Miyake, and Roberto Cavalli. Free alterations. ✆ *2776 Granville St • Map B2 • 604 257 2300*

Left **The Keg Granville Island** Right **Capones Live Jazz Club**

TOP 10 Clubs & Bars

1 AFTERglow Lounge
Sip wine by the glass or boutique beers while nibbling on small skewers of delicacies in this urban lounge. ◈ 1082 Hamilton St • Map K4 • 604 602 0835

2 Richard's on Richards
Ticketed shows by name musicians are followed by open doors to 3am on Fridays and Saturdays for dancing. ◈ 1036 Richards St • Map K4 • 604 687 6794

3 Yaletown Brewing Company
Enjoy locally brewed beer here while dining on homestyle cooking in the pub, the restaurant, or on the historic loading dock. ◈ 1111 Mainland St • Map K5 • 604 681 2739

4 Capones Live Jazz Club
Live jazz seven nights a week and Italian food is a classic match. Extensive wine list and an award-winning martini list. ◈ 1141 Hamilton St • Map J5 • 604 684 7900

5 Bar None
In a converted post-and-beam warehouse, this bar's ambience is urban cool. Live music, a spacious dance floor, and ample seating. ◈ 1222 Hamilton St • Map J5 • 604 689 7000

6 The Yale
Housed in an 1890s railway bunkhouse, The Yale is a no-frills rock and blues hangout, where legendary musicians sometimes play. Nightly live music, pool tables, and a dance floor. ◈ 1300 Granville St • Map J4 • 604 681 9253

7 Dockside Restaurant and Brewing Company
Savor the delicious beer brewed here while admiring the boats on False Creek. Great patio. ◈ Granville Island Hotel, 1253 Johnston St • Map H6 • 604 685 7070

8 Backstage Lounge
This low-key hangout attracts theatergoers and actors from the Granville Island Stage next door. Live music and jams, with a focus on local talent. ◈ 1585 Johnston St • Map H5 • 604 687 1354

9 The Keg Granville Island
The lounge of this steakhouse, known for its "Keg size" caesar – a Canadian concoction of vodka, clamato juice, and spices – is a casual spot for a drink. ◈ 1499 Anderson St • Map H5 • 604 685 4735

10 Sammy J Peppers Bar and Grill
This waterfront bar serves up cold beer and a variety of dishes. Big-screen TV for sports fans. ◈ 1517 Anderson St • Map H5 • 604 696 0739

Around Vancouver – South Granville & Yaletown

Price Categories

For a three-course meal for one with half a bottle of wine (or equivalent meal), taxes and extra charges.

$	under $20
$$	$20–$35
$$$	$35–$60
$$$$	$60–$85
$$$$$	over $85

Above **Dockside patio, Bridges**

🔟 Restaurants

1 Blue Water Café and Raw Bar
Inventive West Coast dishes made with the freshest local fish, and sushi made with coastal shellfish, are masterfully prepared here. Excellent wine list. ◈ 1095 Hamilton St • Map K4 • 604 688 8078 • $$$$

2 C Restaurant
Here, in a sophisticated setting, top chef Robert Clark conjures up the best seafood dishes in town. ◈ 1600 Howe St • Map H5 • 604 681 1164 • $$$$$

3 Il Giardino
The warmly lit dining room and the scrumptious dishes beautifully reflect the heritage of Umberto Menghi, the Tuscan-born owner. Lovely patio. ◈ 1382 Hornby St • Map J4 • 604 669 2422 • $$$$$

4 Cioppino's Mediterranean Grill
Chef "Pino" Posteraro creates delicious lighter versions of traditional Italian pasta, risottos, and seafood dishes. ◈ 1133 Hamilton St • Map J5 • 604 688 7466 • $$$$

5 Provence Marinaside
This restaurant and bar is one of the prettiest places on False Creek. A sommelier is on hand to help select the wine. Picnic baskets available. ◈ 1177 Marinaside Cres • Map K5 • 604 681 4144 • $$$$

6 glowbal grill & satay bar
Spectacular regional dishes such as tuna tartare and grilled veal are prepared in the open kitchen of this trendy restaurant. Superb wine list. ◈ 1079 Mainland St • Map K4 • 604 602 0835 • $$$$

7 Rodney's Oyster House
The action is at the counter, so sidle up and order any of 12 to 20 oyster varieties, shucked as you watch. Steamed clams and mussels, crab, and Atlantic lobster are also featured. ◈ 1228 Hamilton St • Map J5 • 604 609 0080 • $$$$

8 Brix
Pizzas and organic salads mix and match well in this Euro-feel spot. Stellar wine list. ◈ 1138 Homer St • Map J5 • 604 915 9463 • $$$

9 Go Fish!
Wild salmon, halibut, and oysters arrive daily from nearby Fisherman's Wharf. ◈ 1505 W 1st Ave • Map G6 • 604 730 5040 • $$

10 Bridges
Fine dining on grilled salmon, steamed mussels, and steak at the upstairs waterfront restaurant. The bistro downstairs, with its dockside deck, offers more casual fare. ◈ 1696 Duranleau St • Map H5 • 604 687 4400 • $$$

Left **Main Library, University of British Columbia** Right **BC Ferry, Horseshoe Bay**

Greater Vancouver & Beyond

ONE OF THE REASONS *Vancouver* is so often listed among the top ten cities of the world in which to live is the wide range of things to do, and the breathtakingly lovely scenery in which to do them, just a short drive away from the downtown core. Sandy beaches, rugged coastlines, and popular ski hills are minutes away. The ski slopes and golf courses of Whistler are reached after a scenic three-hour drive, ideal for an overnight excursion. Splendid rainforests can be enjoyed in the University of British Columbia's Pacific Spirit Regional Park and in North Vancouver's Capilano Suspension Bridge and Park. Towns such as Squamish or Brackendale provide unforgettable nature walks, hikes and climbs, affording glimpses of the region's flora and fauna. Some small waterfront towns such as Steveston, a former fishing village, have proudly preserved their local history.

Performer, Capilano Suspension Bridge

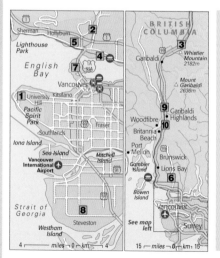

🔟 Sights

1. **University of British Columbia**
2. **Capilano Suspension Bridge and Park**
3. **Whistler**
4. **North Vancouver**
5. **West Vancouver**
6. **Grouse Mountain**
7. **Stanley Park**
8. **Steveston**
9. **Brackendale**
10. **Squamish**

Avoid getting caught in central Vancouver rush hour traffic when making excursions to destinations beyond the city proper **See p105**

Modern fountain, Lonsdale Quay

University of British Columbia

A mix of historic and modern architecture, the buildings of BC's oldest university are complemented by diverse gardens. The campus offers fantastic views across the Strait of Georgia. At the renowned Museum of Anthropology *(see p34)*, visit the First Nations Longhouse, constructed in traditional Coast Salish style in 1993, to admire its four carved houseposts and two carved roof beam ends. The huge Pacific Spirit Regional Park *(see p88)* draws many visitors. ✆ *Map A2 • 604 822 2211 • www.ubc.ca • First Nations Longhouse: 1985 West Mall*

Capilano Suspension Bridge and Park

This North Vancouver park has been around since 1888. Its suspension bridge sways 230 ft (70 m) above the Capilano River *(see pp14–15)*.

Whistler

Two mountains, Whistler and Blackcomb, rise side by side at the resort town of Whistler. Enjoy views of the four villages and surrounding mountains and valleys year round, fog and snow allowing, by way of gondolas and lift chairs *(see pp28–31)*.

North Vancouver

North Vancouver is a busy North Shore city of more than 126,000 residents. Take the scenic SeaBus ride across Burrard Inlet. Disembark at Lonsdale Quay, a public market selling fresh produce, meats, and baked goods, as well as handmade jewelry and crafts. Grab a takeaway from the food court and head for the outdoor seating area. Lynn Canyon Park boasts its own suspension bridge, spanning the dramatic canyon, 165 ft (50 m) above Lynn Creek, as well as 40 types of moss and 100-year-old Douglas firs. Stop in at the Ecology Centre to view the displays and films, and get details on park tours and trails. ✆ *Map B1 • Lynn Canyon Park: at the end of Peters Rd, Lynn Valley • Lynn Canyon Ecology Centre: 604 981 3103*

Skier enjoying the view, Whistler Mountain

The Baden-Powell hiking trail stretches from Horseshoe Bay **(see p86)** *to Deep Cove, and runs through Lynn Canyon Park*

A Convocation of Eagles

Almost half the world's bald eagle population lives in BC. Thousands make their annual winter home in Brackendale. The first eagle count took place along the Squamish River in 1985, when six people counted 500 eagles. Some 2,000 eagles are now counted annually, feasting on spawning chum salmon and sitting in the cottonwood trees, with the best viewing in December and January. Brackendale Winter Eagle Festival takes place every January.

5 West Vancouver

This upscale North Shore community is home to over 42,000 people. Lighthouse Park (see p48), Cypress Provincial Park (see p48), and Horseshoe Bay are among the outdoor attractions here. Horseshoe Bay was once a popular summer spot for Vancouverites, who arrived by train or steamer, and it remains a pleasant day-trip destination. Its small bayside park features two totem poles and a pier. BC Ferries (see p106) depart here for Nanaimo, Bowen Island, and the Sunshine Coast. The pedestrian Centennial Seawall runs between Ambleside Park and charming Dundarave village. For a glimpse into the area's history, visit the West Vancouver Museum & Archives. ◎ Map B1
• West Vancouver Museum & Archives: 680 17th St, 604 925 7295 • Open Sep–Jun: 12pm–4:30pm Tue–Sat; Jun–Sep: 11am–5pm Tue–Sun

6 Grouse Mountain

There's lots to do atop this Vancouver landmark including spotting wildlife and watching logging shows. The Feasthouse invites visitors into a beautifully crafted cedar longhouse to learn about Pacific Northwest First Nations cultures. At night, legends come alive with traditional Native cuisine, song, and dance. ◎ 6400 Nancy Greene Way, North Vancouver • Map F3 • 604 984 0661 • www. grousemountain.com • Adm to Skyride

7 Stanley Park

A 1,000-acre (404-ha) park of tamed wilderness just outside downtown. The perimeter seawall has great views of the harbor and Coast Mountains (see pp8–11).

8 Steveston

Old-fashioned Steveston village was built on the salmon industry, with 15 canneries once employing thousands. The Gulf of Georgia Cannery National Historic Site offers a peek into this past. The converted 1894 building rests on pylons over the Fraser River. View the kid-friendly film inside, then tour the huge building. A children's discovery area is set up in the Ice House. ◎ Map B3 • Gulf of Georgia Cannery: 12138 4th Ave • 604 664 9009 • Closed Nov–Mar • Adm

The village of Steveston on the Fraser River

Brackendale

9 Brackendale is best known for the bald eagles that winter in the nearby 1,900-acre (770-ha) Brackendale Eagles Provincial Park, but its ocean and river location also make this small town a great place for rafting and canoeing. After enjoying a day on the water in summer, or watching the eagles feast on salmon in winter, refuel in Brackendale Art Gallery's cozy teahouse. ◈ *Map E2 • Brackendale Art Gallery: 41950 Government Rd*

The Stawamus Chief, Squamish

Squamish

10 "Squamish," a Coast Salish word meaning "mother of the wind," is an apt name for this windy town that has become a major center for outdoor activities. Rock climbers relish the challenge of the Stawamus Chief, an imposing granite monolith. Others windsurf on the Squamish River or camp in nearby parks, including renowned Garibaldi Provincial Park. Visit the West Coast Heritage Railway Park to see the famed black-and-gold Royal Hudson Steam Train or take a minitrain ride. ◈ *Map E3 • West Coast Heritage Railway Park: 39645 Government Rd • 604 898 9336 • Adm*

A Drive Along the North Shore

Morning

Begin at the Stanley Park end of **Lions Gate Bridge**, where two stone lions will welcome you. Cross the bridge and take the North Vancouver exit onto Marine Drive, making the first left-hand turn onto Capilano Rd. Continue for 10 minutes to **Grouse Mountain**. Parking the car, hop on the Skyride for the 1-mile (1.5-km) ride to the top. Spend 90 minutes visiting the grizzlies at the **Refuge for Endangered Wildlife**, and watching the lumberjack show and **Theatre in the Sky**'s dramatic video on beautiful BC.

Lunch at **Altitudes Bistro**, enjoying marvelous views.

Afternoon

After lunch return to the car and drive down Capilano Rd, about 5 minutes, to **Capilano Suspension Bridge** *(see pp14–15)*. Cross the heart-stopping bridge to **Treetops Adventure** for an eagle's-eye view of the rainforest.

Return to Marine Dr via Capilano Rd, driving west about 15 minutes to 25th St in West Vancouver, then turn left toward **Dundarave Park**. The scenic pier and park at the water's edge marks one end of the **Centennial Seawalk**.

After a breath of fresh sea air, walk up to **Marine Drive** and boutique shopping in Dundarave village.

End the day at one of **The Beach House**'s patio tables *(see p90)*, watching the sun set over Dundarave Beach as you dine.

Brackendale Art Gallery hosts the village's annual eagle festival; call 604 898 3333 for details or visit www.brackendaleartgallery.com

Left **Pacific Spirit Regional Park** Right **VanDusen Botanical Gardens**

Best Greenspaces

1 Stanley Park

Stanley Park is replete with gardens, a seawalk, a rainforest with trails, and swimming pools. Rollerblades and bicycles can be rented near the Denman Street entrance to the park *(see pp8–11)*.

2 Pacific Spirit Regional Park

Trails in this 1,862-acre (754-ha) diverse park, also known as UBC Endowment Lands, are frequented by equestrians, walkers, and cyclists. They're well marked but can be rough going in bad weather. ◈ W 16th Ave at Blanca St • Map A2 • 604 224 5739 • www.gvrd.bc.ca/parks

3 Queen Elizabeth Park

This park at the highest point in Vancouver, 505 ft (167 m) above sea level, offers splendid views and gardens, and a conservatory *(see p38)*. ◈ W 33rd Ave & Cambie St • Map B2 • 604 257 8570 • www.parks.vancouver.bc.ca

4 VanDusen Botanical Garden

Secluded nooks and crannies can still be found at this world-famous garden. Seasonal displays. ◈ 5251 Oak St • Map B2 • 604 878 9274 • www.vandusengarden.org • Adm

5 Grouse Mountain

Walk, bike, hike, snowboard, or ski up the mountain and enjoy a fantastic view of the city once you've reached the top. Challenge yourself with the 2-mile (3-km) Grouse Grind climb to the summit, at 3,973 ft (1,211 m) *(see p86)*.

6 Mount Seymour Provincial Park

Mountaineers and skiers relish the snow and gentle slopes in winter. In summer, hikers come seeking fabulous views. ◈ 1700 Mt Seymour Rd, North Vancouver • Map C1 • 604 986 2261 • www.mountseymour.com

7 Cypress Provincial Park

Cypress Mountain offers sports galore and panoramic views as far as Mount Baker, in Washington State. ◈ Top of Cypress Bowl Rd, West Vancouver • Map E3 • 604 926 5612 • www.cypressmountain.com

8 George C. Reifel Migratory Bird Sanctuary

Snow geese and gyrfalcons are among the 60,000 birds visiting this huge site on Westham Island. View the wetlands from the platforms and hides. ◈ 5191 Robertson Rd • Map E4 • 604 946 6980 • www.reifelbirdsanctuary.com • Adm

9 Lighthouse Park

Giant ferns and huge boulders are signatures of this waterfront park. Quiet trails lead through the area's last remaining stand of old-growth trees.
◈ Marine Dr & Beacon Lane, West Vancouver • Map A1 • 604 925 7275 • www.westvancouver.net

10 West Dyke Trail

This 3.5-mile (5.5-km) trail offers views of Sturgeon Banks, an estuary attracting 1.4 million birds a year as part of the Pacific Flyway. ◈ Map A3 • www.richmond.ca/parksrec

Left **Mountain biker, Squamish area** Right **Whitewater rafting, Fraser River**

10 Adventure Sports

1 Glacier Skiing
Horstman Glacier *(see p28)* offers 112 acres (45 ha) of skiing and incomparable views year-round. Varied terrain gives even experienced skiers plenty of thrills. ⓢ *Whistler Blackcomb: 1 866 218 9690 • www.whistlerblackcomb.com*

2 Heli-Snowboarding
Fly away from the Whistler Blackcomb crowds into the pristine high-alpine powder. Guides help you choose from over 1,000 runs. ⓢ *Great Canadian Adventure: 888 285 1676 • www.adventures.com*

3 Paragliding
Learn to be airborne on a tandem flight with a certified teacher. Coastal winds ensure breathtaking heights. ⓢ *Blue Thermal: 1 800 717 3422 • www.bluethermal.com*

4 Rock Climbing
Squamish is one of the top climbing areas in North America. If you're not ready to tackle Stawamus Chief, a formidable cliff rising 2,139 ft (652 m), try Smoke Bluffs. ⓢ *Squamish Rock Guides: 604 815 1750 • www.squamishrockguides.com*

5 Windsurfing
Windsurfers converge at the mouth of the Squamish River in Howe Sound, where north winds blow at 40 to 70 knots. Squamish Windsurfing Society operates the sailing park and rescue service, and charges a sailing fee. ⓢ *www.squamishwindsurfing. org; Wind line: 604 926 9463*

6 Whitewater Rafting
Paddling or power rafting just two hours from Vancouver in Yale on the Nahatlatch, Thompson, and Fraser rivers. Choice of raft size, trip length, and fright factor. ⓢ *Fraser River Raft Expeditions: 1 800 363 7238 • www.fraserraft.com*

7 Mountain Biking
BC offers unlimited trails and backroads. The 93-mile (150-km) Sea to Sky trail stretches from Squamish to D'Arcy. Find maps and trail ratings on the online Whistler Mountain Bike Guide. ⓢ *www.whistlermountainbike.com*

8 Skydiving
Whether you're experienced or a newcomer to skydiving, the view of the Fraser Valley at 3,000 ft (915 m) is spectacular. First-jump tandem lessons available on weekends and holidays. ⓢ *Fraser Valley Skydiving: 604 794 3483 • www.fvskydiving.com*

9 Diving
Find marine life, deep wall diving spots, a shipwreck, artificial reefs, and unusual geographic formations at Howe Sound's many dive sites. Charters, lessons, and equipment available. ⓢ *Blue Zone Diving: 604 537 1767*

10 Kayaking with Orcas
Paddle alongside an orca pod at Vancouver Island's glacier-carved eastern coastline. ⓢ *Northern Lights Expeditions: 1 800 754 7402 • www.seakayaking.com*

Left **Lumière** Right **West**

TOP 10 Restaurants

1 Bishop's
Chef John Bishop combines intimate dining with flawless service. Organic ingredients determine the weekly West Coast menu. Dinner only. ◉ *2183 W 4th Ave • Map B2 • 604 738 2025 • $$$$$*

2 West
Behind the unassuming doorway lies a spacious interior with sleek decor and contemporary regional fare. Vies for best restaurant in the city. ◉ *2881 Granville St • Map B2 • 604 738 8938 • $$$$$*

3 Salmon House on the Hill
Perched in the North Shore hills, this restaurant is known for its green alderwood-grilled BC salmon. First Nations art and artifacts complement the rustic yet elegant interior of wood and glass. ◉ *2229 Folkstone Way, West Vancouver • Map B1 • 604 926 3212 • $$$$*

4 Cru
Here, the lines of fine dining, lounge, and bistro blur. The menu consists of lovely small plates and a four-course *prix fixe*. Try the luscious steamed mussels, or duck confit and *frisée* salad with warm bacon dressing. ◉ *1459 W Broadway • Map B2 • 604 677 4111 • $$*

5 Bin 942 Tapas Parlour
Delectable, creative tapas. Favorites are clay pot chicken or Angus beef tenderloin in phyllo. The music is lively and so is the crowd. ◉ *1521 W Broadway • Map B2 • 604 734 9421 • $$$*

6 Lumière
Rob Feenie beat TV's Iron Chef in 2005, cinching his position as chef extraordinaire. His menu is classical French. Signature items are roasted sablefish and magret duck. ◉ *2551 W Broadway • Map B2 • 604 739 8185 • $$$$$*

7 The Beach House at Dundarave Pier
Sit on the deck of this 1912 house, choose a glass of wine from the long list, and enjoy West Coast cuisine. ◉ *150 25th St, West Vancouver • Map B1 • 604 922 1414 • $$$*

8 Araxi
Local produce is served with a Mediterranean bent at this low-key yet classy spot. Oysters and wild salmon for fish-lovers, lamb confit and steaks for others. Good wine list. ◉ *4222 Village Sq, Whistler • Map F1 • 604 932 4540 • $$$$$*

9 Trattoria di Umberto
The warmth of Tuscany is reflected in the imaginative pasta dishes of celebrity chef Umberto Menghi. Other highlights include *cioppino* (Italian fish chowder) and lamb shanks. Excellent wine list. ◉ *4417 Sundial Pl, Whistler • Map F1 • 604 932 5858 • $$$$$*

10 Tex Corleone's
Chicken, ribs, and deep-dish pizzas in a room decorated with Old West movie posters. Kids love the coloring pages and cowboy hats. ◉ *4154 Village Green, Whistler • Map F1 • 604 932 5858 • $$$*

 All restaurants accept credit cards and serve vegetarian food unless otherwise stated

Price Categories

For a three-course meal for one with half a bottle of wine (or equivalent meal), taxes and extra charges.

$	under $20
$$	$20–$35
$$$	$35–$60
$$$$	$60–$85
$$$$$	over $85

Above **Vij's**

10 Asian Restaurants

1 Hon's Wun-Tun House
Fast, satisfying Cantonese dishes to eat in or take out. Noted for its noodles, potstickers, and *dim sum*. There's also a vegetarian menu. Several locations. ✆ 408 Sixth St • Map C2 • 604 520 6661 • $$

2 Pink Pearl
Often crowded with Chinese families enjoying outstanding *dim sum*. Dinner specialties include Peking duck. ✆ 1132 E Hastings St • Map B2 • 604 253 4316 • $$$

3 Sami's
A fusion of North American and Indian cuisines, plus warm and attentive service. Try the minted mango and ginger soup, or turkey satchels. ✆ 986 W Broadway • Map B2 • 604 736 8330 • $$$

4 Tojo's
Sushi chef Hidekazu Tojo welcomes you as warmly as he does the many celebrities who adore his cozy restaurant. Sidle up to the counter to watch this showman create delightful concoctions such as Dungeness crab topped with cherry blossoms, the shell serving as the plate. ✆ 202-777 W Broadway • Map B2 • 604 872 8050 • $$$$$

5 Kirin Seafood Restaurant
Enjoy Cantonese, Shanghai, and Szechuan dishes and award-winning *dim sum* at this restaurant popular with families. Excellent service. ✆ Three West Centre, 7900 Westminster Hwy, Richmond • Map B3 • 604 303 8833 • $$$$

6 Vij's
A symphony of wondrous flavors, the dishes are a West Coast adaptation of various Indian cooking styles. Specialties are curries, marinated lamb, short ribs, and duck. Dinner only. ✆ 1480 W 11th Ave • Map B2 • 604 736 6664 • $$$

7 Sun Sui Wah
A stunning interior and an exciting *dim sum* selection. Alaska king crab and roast squab are notable entrées. Cantonese dishes are created with light, finely tuned flavors. ✆ 3888 Main St • Map B2 • 604 872 8822 • $$$

8 Montri's Thai Restaurant
Beef, chicken, and prawn entrees are lovingly sautéed with coconut and turmeric. Smoothly spicy curries. ✆ 3629 W Broadway • Map A2 • 604 738 9888 • $$$

9 Habibi's
Traditional Lebanese cooking in an inviting atmosphere. Vegetarian dishes include *tabouli*, salads, and *loubjeh*, savory green string beans in a marvelous sauté of garlic, carrots, cinnamon, and tomatoes. Enjoy live music on Wednesdays. ✆ 1128 W Broadway • Map B2 • 604 732 7487 • $$$

10 The Mekong
Spicy Vietnamese dishes with French and Thai influences served in a small but pleasant room. The pumpkin soup is a must. ✆ 1414 Commercial Dr • Map B2 • 604 253 7088 • $$

Following pages **The Fairmont Empress Hotel on Victoria's Inner Harbour**

Left **Legislative chamber, BC Parliament Buildings** Right **Entrance, Fairmont Empress Hotel**

Victoria

PICTURESQUE, PEACEFUL VICTORIA *is the perfect getaway from bustling Vancouver. Known as the City of Flowers, it boasts more than 3,000 hanging baskets along its pretty streets. Established as a fort in 1843 by the Hudson's Bay trading company, Victoria soon became a city of prestige and influence. It grew up around Beacon Hill Park, created in 1858 by Governor James Douglas. When Victoria became BC's capital in 1868, the growing city attracted excellent architects such as Francis Mawson Rattenbury. Today the city buzzes around the Inner Harbour. Nearby is the oldest Chinatown in Western Canada, the Art Gallery of Greater Victoria, and the home of Victoria's most famous artist, Emily Carr.*

Shrine detail, Art Gallery of Greater Victoria

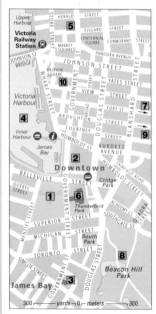

🔟 Sights

1. British Columbia Parliament Buildings
2. Fairmont Empress Hotel
3. Emily Carr House
4. Inner Harbour
5. Chinatown
6. Royal British Columbia Museum
7. Art Gallery of Greater Victoria
8. Beacon Hill Park
9. Craigdarroch Castle
10. Maritime Museum of British Columbia

Shops, Chinatown

1 British Columbia Parliament Buildings

Impressive, gray granite buildings house the provincial legislature. Overlooking the Inner Harbour, they were completed in 1898 by a newcomer, 25-year-old Francis Mawson Rattenbury from Leeds, England. At night, the Neo-Classical structure is a wonderful sight, lit by 3,300 sparkling light bulbs. ◎ *501 Belleville St • Map N4–P4 • 250 387 3046 • Open Jun–Sep: 8:30am–5pm daily; Oct–May: Mon–Fri 8:30am–5pm • www.legis.gov.bc.ca*

2 Fairmont Empress Hotel

The luxury château-style landmark hotel *(see p116)* overlooking the Inner Harbour was designed by Rattenbury and built by the Canadian Pacific Railway in 1908. It is done up in grand style, with towering brick walls partially covered in ivy. The Crystal Ballroom shows off 18 crystal chandeliers and a mirrored ceiling. ◎ *721 Government St • Map P4 • 250 384 8111*

3 Emily Carr House

Built in 1864, the Carr family home typifies the sensibilities of the Victorian era. The architecture has been described as both English Gingerbread and San Francisco Victorian, inspiring the restoration of many of the area's

Emily Carr House

old houses. Emily Carr, one of Canada's best-known artists and writers *(see p19)*, was born here in 1871. Step into the formal dining room to see the Carrs' public face, then visit the crowded upstairs bedrooms, reflecting everyday life. ◎ *207 Government St • Map P6 • 250 383 5843 • Open May & Sep: 11am–4pm Tue–Sat; Jun–Aug: 11am–4pm daily • Adm • www.emilycarr.com*

4 Inner Harbour

The Inner Harbour is the historic center of Victoria. A mix of yachts, fishing boats, ferries, and float planes dock here, while pedestrians happily stroll along a wide, curved walkway. The harbor provides excellent views of the historic parliament buildings and the imposing Fairmont Empress Hotel. ◎ *Map N3*

Fairmont Empress Hotel, facing Inner Harbour

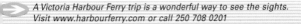

A Victoria Harbour Ferry trip is a wonderful way to see the sights. Visit www.harbourferry.com or call 250 708 0201

Governor James Douglas

James Douglas, known as the father of British Columbia, was born in Demerara, British Guiana (now Guyana), in 1803. His father was a Scottish merchant, his mother a free mulatto. Douglas married Amelia Connolly, the half-Native daughter of a fur trader. Working for the Hudson's Bay Company, Douglas established Fort Victoria in 1843. Over the next 20 years, Governor Douglas transformed Victoria into a center of political power, but he is best remembered as having established Beacon Hill Park, in 1858. Douglas retired in 1863. A knighthood followed. Sir James Douglas died in Victoria in 1877, at the age of 74.

Gallery, Royal British Columbia Museum

5 Chinatown

Victoria's Chinatown once rivaled San Francisco's for size. Today it's an eclectic two-block area, signaled by the ornate Gate of Harmonious Interest. Chinatown was known as the Forbidden City by the European populace of the day. Once notorious Fan Tan Alley, said to be the narrowest street in Canada, hid gambling dens and a thriving opium industry. Today, restaurants, groceries, artists' studios, and souvenir shops fill the bustling streets of this designated heritage area. ◈ *Fisgard & Herald sts at Government St • Map P1*

6 Royal British Columbia Museum

Known for its Native artifacts and art, and displays highlighting BC's history and natural wonders, the museum has excellent exhibits ranging from prehistory to the First Peoples Gallery. A National Geographic IMAX theater, Thunderbird Park, and Helmcken House are on the site *(see pp24–5)*.

7 Art Gallery of Greater Victoria

Housed in an 1889 mansion, this gallery is known for its Asian collection, including a Shinto shrine in the Asian garden. Paintings and literary work by local artist Emily Carr *(see p19)* are another highlight. ◈ *1040 Moss St • 250 384 4101 • Open 10am–5pm daily (to 9pm Thu) • Adm*

8 Beacon Hill Park

Noted for its gnarled Garry oak trees and 350-year-old Chinese bell, the park, dating from the mid-1800s, is a lovely place to stroll and picnic. Over 2,000 varieties of plants and trees, a rose garden, wooden bridges, and stream. ◈ *Map Q6 • 250 361 0600*

Gate of Harmonious Interest, Chinatown

French Gothic tower, Craigdarroch Castle

9 Craigdarroch Castle

This four-story stone mansion was built in the late 1880s for coal baron Robert Dunsmuir, who died soon after it was completed, leaving wife Joan and 11 children to squabble over the estate. Its 39 rooms each exude turn-of-the-19th-century elegance. Highlights include period furnishings, stained glass windows, a sandstone fireplace, and a grand white oak staircase. The views of the ocean and mountains from the tower are magnificent. ◈ *1050 Joan Cres • 250 592 5323 • Open mid-Jun–Labour Day: 9am–7pm daily; Labour Day–mid-June: 10am–4:30pm daily • Adm*

10 Maritime Museum of British Columbia

Three floors of coastal history include the stories of the giant canoes of the Coast Salish First Peoples, the tall ships of the first European explorers, and pirate ships and whalers. Tumultuous tales of coastal shipwrecks are gruesomely fascinating. On the top floor is the former courtroom of notorious Matthew Baillie Begbie, known as the Hanging Judge. The 19th-century courtroom is preserved in all its glory. ◈ *28 Bastion Sq • Map P2 • 250 385 4222 • Open 9:30–4:30pm daily • Adm*

Walking tour of Victoria

Morning

🕐 Starting at the corner of Wharf and Government, stroll 10 minutes north on **Government Street**. Shops along the way include some suitably British purveyors.

At Fisgard St, the colorful **Gate of Harmonious Interest** welcomes you to to Chinatown. Explore the area for an hour, dipping into tiny **Fan Tan Alley**, off Fisgard St. Continue west to Wharf St, then on to **Bastion Square**, the heart of **Old Town**, where fur traders boozed and brawled in the days of Fort Victoria.

The **Maritime Museum of British Columbia** is in a dignified former courthouse on the square. Devote an hour to its displays before heading to **Irish Times Pub**, 1200 Government St, for tasty fish and chips.

Afternoon

Admire the marine traffic from the **Inner Harbour** promenade. At the far end of the harbor, cross **Belleville Street** to the statue of a youthful Queen Victoria on the grounds of the **BC Parliament Buildings**. The fascinating **Royal British Columbia Museum** next door will take at least two hours to peruse.

Exit the museum on the east side to admire the totems in **Thunderbird Park** before checking out nearby historic Helmcken House. Cross Belleville St to the **Fairmont Empress Hotel** for a glimpse of the grandiose lobby.

Replenish with dinner or a drink on the deck of **Milestone's**, 812 Wharf St.

Left **silk road aromatherapy & tea company** Right **Hill's Native Arts**

TOP 10 Shopping

1 British Importers
High-end shop featuring men's off-the-rack sportswear, suits, and accessories with German, Italian, and Canadian brand names; also women's sportswear. ◈ 960 Yates St • 250 386 1496

2 Smoking Lily
Vertical space in this closet-sized shop makes for unusual displays. T-shirts, scarves, bags, and more, all screen-printed by hand. ◈ 569a Johnson St • Map P2 • 250 382 5459

3 Breeze
Mid-priced women's clothing, shoes, and accessories, with three main lines: Kenzie, Mac & Jac, and Mexx. Jewelry by Vancouver designer Soul Flower. ◈ 1150 Government St • Map P2 • 250 383 8871

4 silk road aromatherapy & tea company
The creation of two women who learned the Chinese tea tradition from tea masters and herbalists, silk road boasts, in addition to tea, a spa (see p57) and its own line of natural body care products.
◈ 1624 Government St
• Map P1
• 250 704 2688

5 She She Bags
Hundreds of purses crowd the shop: Madagascan strawbags, bags made of recycled juice containers from a Filipino women's cooperative, and bags with pictures of Marily and Audrey. ◈ 616 View St • Map F • 250 388 0613

6 Hill's Native Arts
Peruse the work of over 1,00 First Nations artists: Northwest Coast and Inuit carvings and print hand-carved jewelry. ◈ 1008 Government St • Map P3 • 250 385 391

7 Fan Tan Gallery
Gifts from around the world, with a focus on India, Indonesia, China, and France. Home accessories include mats, iron sconces baskets, linens, bath products, ar and curios. ◈ 541 Fisgard St • Map P1 • 250 382 4424

8 All in Bloom
Home luxuries and kitschy gifts. Lovely Canadian-made jew elry at affordable prices. ◈ 616 Trounce Alley • Map P2 • 250 383 188

9 Gloss Beauty Bar
Hot trends from France, Italy Canada, and the US, among thousands of beauty products. ◈ 1002 Broad St • Map P3 • 250 418 1002

10 Fort Street Antiques
Discover one-of-a-kind silverware, glass and china, fine art, furniture, and jewelry on Antique Row. ◈ Fort St between Douglas St & Linden Ave • Map Q3

Above **Empress Room, Fairmont Empress Hotel**

10 Restaurants & Cafés

1 Fairmont Empress Hotel
A variety of colonial-themed dining venues await at Victoria's grandest hotel. Especially popular is the formal afternoon tea, served daily since 1908 – reservations are required. ◈ *721 Government St • Map P4 • 250 384 8111 • $$$*

2 Café Brio
Contemporary West Coast food prepared with a Tuscan touch. Menu changes daily, but don't be surprised to find homemade ravioli, spring salmon, and braised halibut or pork belly. Terrific patio. ◈ *944 Fort St • 250 383 0009 • $$$*

3 Spinnakers Brewpub
This is Canada's oldest licensed brewpub. The waterfront dining room menu includes all-natural smoked meats and sausages, perfect companions to the great assortment of beers on tap. ◈ *308 Catherine St • 250 386 2739 • $$$*

4 Canoe
Local organic produce, meat, and wild seafood are on offer at this brewpub, marina, and restaurant, in an historic 1894 waterfront property. Classics such as burgers and fries go especially well with a craft brew. ◈ *450 Swift St • Map N1 • 250 361 1940 • $$$*

5 Brasserie L'École
French bistro dishes – lamb shank, mussels, and *frites* – using local products. ◈ *1715 Government St • Map P1 • 250 475 6260 • $$$*

6 Camille's
Fine West Coast dining in a romantic room. An award-winning menu highlights local organic and regional items. ◈ *45 Bastion Sq • Map P2 • 250 381 3433 • $$$*

7 Il Terrazzo Ristorante
Fine Northern Italian food; heated courtyard. Wood oven-roasted meats and pizzas, pastas, and seafood arrive with a flourish. ◈ *555 Johnson St • Map P2 • 250 361 0028 • $$$*

8 Pagliacci's
Linguine, lasagna, and fettuccine are simple and satisfying. Pag's bread is coveted. ◈ *1011 Broad St • Map P3 • 250 386 1662 • $$$*

9 The Noodle Box
Huge portions of noodle and rice dishes come in decorative boxes, at eight levels of spiciness. ◈ *818 Douglas St • Map P3 • 250 384 1314 • $*

10 Wild Saffron Bistro
Progressive West Coast cuisine including fondues, rack of lamb, seafood, and vegetarian entrées. ◈ *506 Pandora Ave • Map P1 • 250 361 3310 • $$$*

Left **Orca, Gulf Islands** Right **Mural depicting local history, Chemainus**

Excursions from Victoria

1 Nanaimo

The Old Quarter, built during the days when Nanaimo was a coal-mining town, has many 19th-century buildings, including the 1895 Nanaimo Court House. Stroll along the Harbourfront Walkway, stopping at The Bastion military museum, where guards perform daily. Departure Bay has a good beach and public market. Nanaimo is a good starting point for wildlife tours. *Map D4*

2 Cowichan Valley

This pastoral valley is a mix of forests and farmland. Local wines, ciders, and gourmet cheeses attract gastronomically minded visitors by car and touring bicycles. Cowichan Lake is Vancouver Island's main freshwater lake and a terrific spot for swimming, canoeing, and fishing. The Cowichan River is a designated heritage treasure, famed for its fly fishing. *Map D5*

Evergreen forests, Cowichan Valley

3 Chemainus

When the sawmill, the basis of its economy, closed in 1983, Chemainus transformed itself into a picturesque seaside town. More than 35 giant murals by local and international artists appear throughout the town, depicting the region's history. *Map D5*

4 Gulf Islands

Visitors flock to these islands in the Strait of Georgia to enjoy their quietness and natural beauty. Salt Spring with its many artists' studios, and Galiano, which has a lovely provinical park, are the most popular island destinations. Saturna, Pender, Mayne, and Gabriola are the other major islands. Each has its own personality; all are accessible by BC Ferries from Swartz Bay *(see p107)*. *Map E5*

5 Duncan

Duncan is known as the City of Totems for the 80 Coast Salish poles displayed around town. At the Quw'utsun' Cultural Centre see carvers at work, and some of the best Native arts and crafts in BC. The focus of the BC Forest Discovery Centre is the province's heyday of logging. In summer, a 1920s steam train carries passengers past heritage buildings and through a rainforest. *Map E5*
• *Quw'utsun' Cultural Centre: 200 Cowichan Way • 250 746 8119 • Open daily • BC Forest Discovery Centre: 2892 Drinkwater Rd • 250 715 1113 • Open summer: 10am–6pm daily; spring & fall: 10am–4pm daily • Adm*

For information about an excursion to the Long Beach area **See pp26–7**

6 Butchart Gardens
For over a century, the incomparable Butchart Gardens, wrung out of a worked-out quarry, have awed visitors with their lush and varied beauty *(see p38)*. ◈ *800 Benvenuto Ave, Brentwood Bay • Map E5 • 250 652 5256 • Open Jun–Sep: 9am–10:30pm daily; otherwise closing times vary • Adm*

7 Broken Group Islands
An archipelago of some 100 rugged islands and islets is paradise for nature lovers, kayakers, and scuba divers. The area around Barkley Sound has outstanding views of coastal rainforest, beaches, and sea caves. Accessible only by boat, a guided tour is the best way to experience this isolated wilderness. Jamie's Whaling Station in Tofino offers harbor and specialty tours. ◈ *Map B5 • Jamie's Whaling Station: 250 725 3919 • Vancouver Island Kayak: 250 480 9409*

8 Parksville
Parksville's beautiful Rathtrevor Beach is easily accessible for a bevy of waterside sports and activities. Dip your toes in the gentle surf, build sandcastles, dig clams, canoe, or camp along the 4 miles (7 km) of sand. Swim in the warmest saltwater north of California. Nearby are mini-golf courses, bistros, and numerous art studios for one-of-a-kind souvenirs. ◈ *Map C4*

9 Qualicum Beach
Beachcombers and kayakers find delightful Qualicum Beach and its nearby British-style village a pedestrian-friendly stopover. The curved beach overlooking the Strait of Georgia presents magnificent sunsets. ◈ *Map C4*

Victoria's Butchart Gardens

10 Goldstream Provincial Park
Massive old-growth Douglas firs, some 600 years old, tower overhead in this mystic rainforest only 12 mi (19 km) from Victoria. Once a fishing ground for the Coast Salish, miners overran the park during the Gold Rush of the late 1850s *(see p17)*. An annual fall salmon run on the Goldstream River attracts hundreds of majestic bald eagles. Dropping 155 ft (48 m) into a canyon pool, the park's waterfall is easily reached by a five-minute walk along a trail. A visitor house offers a variety of weekend activities. ◈ *Map E6 • Freeman King Visitor Centre: 2930 Trans Canada Hwy • 250 478 9414 • Open 9am–4:30pm daily*

See Vancouver Island aboard the Malahat train, running from Victoria to Courtenay, and alight as often as you like; visit www.viarail.ca

101

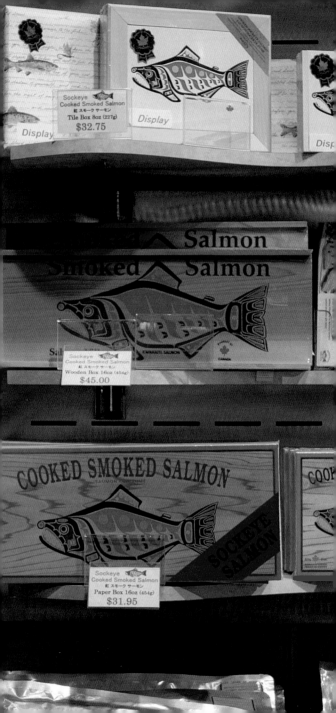

Sockeye
Cooked Smoked Salmon
紅 スモーク サーモン
Tile Box 8oz (227g)
$32.75

Display

Display

Display

Salmon

Smoked ◆ Salmon

Sockeye
Cooked Smoked Salmon
紅 スモーク サーモン
Wooden Box 16oz (454g)
$45.00

CANADA

COOKED SMOKED SALMON

SOCKEYE SALMON

Sockeye
Cooked Smoked Salmon
紅 スモーク サーモン
Paper Box 16oz (454g)
$31.95

COO

STREETSMART

VANCOUVER & VICTORIA'S TOP 10

Left **Winter skiing, Whistler Mountain** Right **Blooms of spring, Queen Elizabeth Park**

Planning Your Trip

1 When to Go

Vancouver and Victoria's temperate coastal climate is best from April to November. Rain falls intermittently from November to March. In the city and along the coast, winter temperatures rarely drop below freezing. Temperatures are lower in the mountains and, to the delight of skiers at resorts such as Whistler, there is snow. Summer can be hot but the nights are cooler.

2 What to Pack

Pack a warm sweater and a light jacket in late spring and early fall. In late fall and early spring, pack a heavier jacket or coat, and two warm sweaters. In winter, pack a hat, scarf, gloves, warm coat, and waterproof boots. A light sweater or blazer, cotton or linen dresses, slacks, shorts and T-shirts are ideal for summer; sunglasses, sunscreen, and an umbrella are a must.

3 Health Insurance

Unless your health insurance covers medical costs while traveling, buying comprehensive health and dental insurance is strongly recommended: Canada does not provide free medical services to visitors. Many credit card companies provide some degree of insurance; it is worthwhile to check this out before your trip.

4 Passports & Visas

A valid travel document, usually a passport, combined with a visa when needed, must be presented by visitors upon entry to Canada. Residents of many countries, such as the US, Australia, Ireland, New Zealand, and the majority of European countries, including Britain, do not need a visa. Visitors may remain in Canada for up to six months.

5 Customs

Canada's rules governing what can be brought into the country are complex. In general, do not bring live animals, fresh fruit, vegetables, meat, dairy products, plants, or firearms into Canada without first obtaining authorization. Limited amounts of alcohol and tobacco may be imported duty-free by visitors who are of age (19 and 18 years old, respectively). Upon entry into Canada, you must declare any cash amount equal to or more than Can\$10,000.

6 Driver's License

Driver's licenses from the US and from other countries are valid in BC for up to six months. If you plan on staying longer, an International Driving Permit (obtained in your home country), combined with your license, will allow you to drive in the province for up to a year.

7 Car Insurance

Insurance coverage for drivers is mandatory in BC. If you are renting a car, check your policy before leaving home to see if it covers a rental car. Most rental agencies offer damage and liability insurance; it is a good idea to have both. Some credit cards include car insurance coverage.

8 Electricity

Canada uses a 110-volt, 60-cycle electrical system. Electrical sockets accept two- or three-pronged plugs. Bring a plug adapter and a voltage transformer to run appliances and cell-phone chargers that are not manufactured in North America or that don't have an optional voltage switch.

9 Time Zone

Vancouver is in the Pacific Time zone (eight hours behind Greenwich Mean Time). Daylight Savings Time begins the first Sunday in April when clocks are turned forward one hour, and ends in late October when clocks are turned back one hour.

10 Discounts

Most movie theaters, major attractions, and public transit systems offer reduced rates for people over age 65. Students are eligible for many discounts with ID. Hotels also often offer discounts, but only if you ask for them.

Contact the Canadian embassy or High Commission nearest you for entry requirements, or visit www.cic.gc.ca/english/visit

Left **Downtown crowds** Right **Pre-paid parking area**

TOP 10 Things to Avoid

1 Leaving Valuables in Cars
Vancouver is notorious for thefts from cars. Leave nothing visible in your vehicle and take all valuables with you, including documents. If you shop, don't assume putting purchases in your car's trunk will keep them safe: thieves may spot you storing bags in the trunk and steal them when you continue shopping.

2 Hotel Telephone Calls
Avoid making long-distance calls from your hotel room that are charged directly to hotel bills – they are at least three times more expensive than using a phone card. You can buy a pre-paid phone card at convenience stores and newsstands. Local calls may be free from your room, or there may be a charge. Ask before you call out as this can add up.

3 Rush Hour
The best way to deal with rush hour traffic in Vancouver is to avoid it entirely. From 3:30pm to 6:00pm traffic slows or even comes to a complete halt. In the morning, wait until 9:30am before driving. Don't underestimate your driving time. Rush hour in Victoria is lighter.

4 Driving in Cities
Since many attractions in Vancouver and Victoria are within walking distance, or are an easy bus ride away, it makes sense to leave your car at the hotel. If you are thinking of renting a vehicle to travel further afield, check the alternatives first, such as public transit, which even offers shuttle buses to Whistler in ski season *(see p107)*.

5 Tickets
Obey the speed limits posted on city streets. Speeding tickets are costly in BC. In pre-paid parking areas, make sure to buy ample time. Parking tickets come swiftly and are an unwelcome drain on your budget.

6 Pickpockets
A pickpocket looks just like any other person, so be watchful of people bumping into you – it could be a thief at work. A favorite trick of pickpockets is to work the crowds during the area's many festivals so be particularly careful at these events. Bus stops are notorious. Keep your valuables close to your body under your outer garments *(see p111)*.

7 Dangerous Areas
Vancouver is generally a safe city but as with any big city, caution is advised. The Theatre District downtown can be the scene of rowdy behavior. The downtown eastside around Hastings and Main streets, and west on Hastings from Main to Cambie, is known for drug dealers. Take a bus or taxi to and from Chinatown along Pender Street to avoid this section. Finally, avoid all parks after dark. Crime rates in Victoria are low, though panhandlers may prove a nuisance.

8 Airport Con Artists
Disoriented travelers are easy targets for con artists and thieves. Never travel with large amounts of money or precious jewelry. Avoid taxi drivers who walk up to you offering a ride; take a licensed cab at the taxi stand or a limousine with set rates.

9 Panhandlers
Panhandlers face legal restrictions in BC, but many still appear in various locales. At stoplights, some offer to wash windshields for money. The cities of Vancouver and Victoria discourage giving money to panhandlers.

10 Prostitutes
Prostitutes of both sexes ply their trade in Vancouver, especially in the downtown eastside. Often they are working to support a drug habit and are at a higher risk of being infected with HIV/AIDS than is the general population. The city is trying to improve the lives of prostitutes, and to better control prostitution, but their number remains high.

If you are cycling around Vancouver or Victoria, make sure to lock your bike securely when you take a break

Streetsmart

Left **Airplane taking off from Vancouver Airport** Right **Traffic, downtown Vancouver**

🔟 Arriving in Vancouver & Victoria

1 Main Airports
Vancouver's international airport has two terminals, one for Canadian destinations, one for international. Victoria's airport has one terminal for all flights. Free baggage carts are available at both airports. 🌐 *Vancouver Airport info: 604 207 7077, www.yvr.com • Victoria Airport info: 250 953 7500, www.cyyj.ca*

2 Immigration
Cards to be filled out for immigration and customs are distributed on international flights. On arrival, the immigration officer will ask to see your passport or other ID, and may pose additional questions.

3 Connections from Vancouver International Airport
Vancouver airport is 15 mi (24 km) south of downtown Vancouver. Public buses, taxis, limousines, and car rentals are available at the airport. The Airporter express bus departs every 15 minutes for major Vancouver hotels, the cruise ship terminal *(see p12)*, and the inter-city bus depot. The No. 424 bus picks up on Level 1 of the domestic terminal for Airport Station, by the Delta Hotel. From there, buses depart for Vancouver, Richmond, and beyond. 🌐 *Airporter bus: 1 800 668 3141 • TransLink: 604 946 8866, www.translink.bc.ca*

4 Connections from Victoria International Airport
Located 14 mi (22 km) north of Victoria, the airport is serviced by public transit (route No. 70), taxis, limousines and cars for hire. The AKAL Airport Shuttle departs every 30 minutes for major Victoria hotels. 🌐 *Victoria Regional Transit: 250 382 6161 • AKAL Shuttle: 250 386 2525*

5 Car Rental
At Vancouver airport, most car rental companies have booths on the ground floor of the airport parking garage. If you are driving downtown, note that a section of Granville Street is closed to private vehicles; signs direct you to side streets. Victoria's airport is serviced by several car rental companies.

6 Long-Distance Buses
Greyhound buses arrive from the US and elsewhere in Canada at Pacific Central Station (1150 Station St, Vancouver). 🌐 *Greyhound: 604 482 8747 or 1 800 661 8647 • www.greyhound.ca*

7 Flights from Downtown Vancouver
From the tiny downtown Coal Harbour Airport, West Coast Air links Vancouver to Victoria; Baxter Aviation flies to Nanaimo. Harbour Air Seaplanes services the Gulf Islands. HeliJet operates 12-seat helicopters, with daily service to Victoria. 🌐 *West Coast Air: 604 606 6888 • Baxter Aviation: 1 800 661 5599 • Harbour Air: 604 274 1277 • HeliJet International: 1 800 665 4354*

8 By Rail
Trains arrive at Pacific Central Station in Vancouver, at 1150 Station St. VIA Rail trains arrive from points in Canada. Amtrak's Cascades route links Eugene and Portland, Oregon, and Seattle, Washington, to Vancouver with daily trains. 🌐 *VIA Rail: 1 888 842 7245, www.viarail.ca • Amtrak: 1 800 872 7245, www.amtrak.com*

9 By Water
Many ferry services connect Seattle with Vancouver and Victoria and BC Ferries connects Vancouver with Victoria, the Gulf Islands, and Nanaimo. Cruise ships dock at Canada Place *(see p61)*. Pleasure boats dock at the many marinas in the region; call Tourism BC for details. 🌐 *BC Ferries: 1 888 223 3779, www. bcferries.com • Tourism BC: 1 800 435 5622*

10 By Road
Washington state's I-5 connects with Hwy 99 at the BC border; this leads to Vancouver and Whistler. BC's main Canada-US border crossing is the Peace Arch in Blaine, Washington.

Vancouver and BC bus schedules are available for free at Vancouver airport's customer service counters, Arrivals level

Left **Vancouver's SkyTrain** Right **Taxi in front of the Opus Hotel, Vancouver**

Getting Around Vancover & Victoria

1 Buses & SeaBus
Public transit (Translink) bus routes extend across Greater Vancouver. Ask the driver for a transfer so you can switch to the SkyTrain or SeaBus – catamarans that cross the harbor in a short 12 minutes. The Victoria Regional Transit System operates a large network of buses across Victoria. Ⓢ *Vancouver route info: 604 953 3333* • *www.translink.bc.ca* • *Victoria route info: 250 382 6161*

2 SkyTrain
Vancouver's SkyTrain is an above-ground light rapid transit system. Tickets are also transfers. They are good for 90 minutes, and valid for round trips and connections to buses and the SeaBus.

3 Transit Fares
Vancouver's TransLink system has three fare zones, but on weekdays after 6:30pm and weekends, the system reverts to one zone. Victoria's transit system has two fare zones. In both cities, bus drivers do not sell tickets or provide change. If you don't have a ticket, pay the exact cash fare when boarding. Sheets or books of 10 tickets and day passes are money-savers. These are sold at SkyTrain stations (Vancouver) and at many convenience stores and supermarkets. People with disabilities, children

5 to 13 years, seniors and students with proper ID are eligible for concession fares. Children under 4 years ride free in Vancouver, under 6 in Victoria, where family savings are also available using daypasses.

4 Taxis
Flagging a taxi on Vancouver city streets is easy – cabs are plentiful. In Victoria, fewer taxis cruise the streets, so it is best to order a cab by phone.

5 Ferries
Ferries to Victoria and the Gulf Islands depart from Tsawwassen; those to Nanaimo, the Sunshine Coast, and Bowen Island leave from Horseshoe Bay. All ferries carry bicycles for a fee. Car reservations, also for a fee, are advised for peak periods. Ⓢ *Ferry info: 1 888 223 3779 in BC; 250 386 3431 outside BC* • *www.bcferries.com*

6 Walking
Walking is the best way to explore downtown Vancouver and Victoria. Streets are fairly safe *(see p105)*. The south arm of the False Creek seawalk *(see p71)* leads from Vanier Park *(see p78)* past several beaches to Spanish Banks, UBC *(see p85)*, and beyond. In Victoria, a walk on the promenade along the Inner Harbour offers excellent views of historic buildings and the harbor *(see p95)*.

7 HandyDART
Both Victoria and Vancouver operate a shared-ride service for people unable to use public transit. Pre-register at least 10 days ahead of your trip. Ⓢ *HandyDART: Vancouver, 604 430 2692, Victoria: 250 727 9607*

8 Cycling
Cyclists must follow the same rules of the road as drivers. Bikes may not be ridden on sidewalks, and wearing a helmet is mandatory. Bikes are allowed on Vancouver's SkyTrain and SeaBus in non-peak hours. Buses in both cities offer bike racks on many routes.

9 Driving
A good map is essential, especially in Vancouver. Hwys 1 and 99 can be very busy during rush hour *(see p105)*. There are no freeways by-passing the city core. Speed limits are posted. Right-hand turns on red lights are legal throughout BC unless otherwise posted.

10 Boat Tours
For boat tours of Howe Sound and Victoria Harbour, check with the tourist information centers in Vancouver and Victoria. Ⓢ *Touristinfo Centre Vancouver: Plaza Level, 200 Burrard St, 604 683 2000, www.tourismvancouver.com* • *Tourism Victoria: 812 Wharf St, 250 953-2033, www.tourismvictoria.com*

Streetsmart

Left **Free outdoor activities, English Bay** Right **Inexpensive cruise, SeaBus ferry**

🔟 Budget Tips

1 Attractions Discounts
Save up to 40 percent on tickets to popular Vancouver attractions by buying tickets in advance from the Vancouver Touristinfo Centre. In Victoria, discount coupon books are available from Tourism Victoria. ❧ *Vancouver: 200 Burrard St, 604 683 2000 • Victoria: 31 Bastion Sq, 250 414 6999*

2 Budget Shopping
Look for inexpensive, unusual souvenirs in Chinatown and in the shops along Commercial Drive *(see p55)*, brimming with ethnic goods. Visit Main Street for second-hand bargains and one-of-a-kind designer wear on a budget. In Victoria, you can spend hours browsing through the collectibles at the Capital Iron (1900 Store St), then stop next door at Value Village (1810 Store St) for rock-bottom prices on used clothing and housewares.

3 Savings on the Go
Save on public transit costs in Vancouver and Victoria by buying all-zone day passes, or books of ten tickets for the price of eight *(see p107)*.

4 Outdoor Activities
Vancouver and Victoria's year-round mild weather makes outdoor activities especially appealing. From a stroll along Stanley Park's paths *(see pp8–9)* to the tough

Grouse Grind climb *(see p88)*, Vancouver has hiking trails for all fitness levels. Or rent a bike, buy a kite, or grab your binoculars and birder's guide and head to the beach. In Victoria, the Inner Harbour walkway *(see p95)* provides free entertainment and exercise.

5 Low-Cost Literary
There are plenty of affordable literary events in Vancouver and Victoria. Check the listings in the *Vancouver Sun*'s Queue section, the free *Georgia Straight* weekly, and the free *Monday Magazine* in Victoria. Libraries, bookshops, and cafés often host readings and poetry slams. For book bargains, visit Book Warehouse in Vancouver and Munro's in Victoria *(see p112)*.

6 Free or Reduced Admission Days
Admission to the Vancouver Art Gallery *(see pp18–19)* is by donation on Thursdays, from 5 to 9pm. UBC Museum of Anthropology *(see p34)* is free Tuesdays after 5pm. The BC Parliament Buildings in Victoria *(see p95)* offer free guided tours from late May to September.

7 Show Discounts
Tickets Tonight sells half-price tickets at the Touristinfo Centre for Vancouver shows the day of the performance. Some theaters offer two-for-one tickets to matinees and

previews; be sure to ask. Vancouver Playhouse *(see p42)* sells discount tickets one hour before show time. The Victoria Symphony offers ticket discounts with a receipt from certain restaurants. ❧ *Vancouver Touristinfo Centre: 200 Burrard St, 604 683 2000 • Victoria Symphony, 250 385 6515*

8 Cut-Rate Cruises
Rides on BC Ferries are inexpensive mini-cruises. Particularly lovely is the route to the southern Gulf Islands. In Vancouver, if you have only an hour to spare, hop on the SeaBus or any False Creek ferry *(see p107)*. ❧ *BC Ferries: 1 888 223 3779 • www.bcferries.bc.ca*

9 Cheap Eats
It's easy to find good-quality but bargain Asian food in Vancouver. In Victoria, head to Chinatown for deals. Or buy a hot dog and pretzel from a street-vendor. You can also save by opting for a picnic lunch in a park.

10 Campus Deals
Both Simon Fraser University and the University of British Columbia *(see p85)* put on free or inexpensive concerts, lectures, and other events. Admission is cheap to Cinecenta's second-run movies, at the University of Victoria. Visit the websites for listings. ❧ *www.sfu.ca • www.ubc.ca • www.cinecenta.com*

 In summer, the Architectural Institute of BC offers walking tours of Victoria and Vancouver for $5; call 604 683 8588 or visit www.aibc.ca

Left **Vancouver Trolley tour** Right **Touristinfo Centre sign, Vancouver**

10 Excursion Tips

1 Walking Tours
Learn more about Vancouver's Chinatown with guides from the Chinese Cultural Centre. Historic Gastown comes alive in Gastown Business Improvement Society (GBIS) tours. Walkabout Historic Vancouver has professional guides who lead tours of downtown, Granville Island, and Gastown. ✪ Chinese Cultural Centre: 604 658 8880 • GBIS: 604 683 5650 • Walkabout Historic Vancouver: 604 720 0006

2 Trolley Tours
Classic trolley cars are replicated in modern sightseeing buses. The year-round city tour is two hours, but you can hop on or off at any of the 23 stops. ✪ Vancouver Trolley: 604 801 5515

3 Rail Tours
Rail travel is a Canadian classic. VIA Rail transcontinental service guarantees cozy sleepers, fine cuisine, and attentive staff. Rocky Mountaineer vacations offers spectacular packages, such as a famed two-day, all daylight trip between Vancouver and the Rockies. ✪ Rocky Mountaineer Vacations: 604 606 7245 or 1 800 665 7245 • VIA Rail: 1 888 842 7245

4 Bus Tours
Gray Line's luxurious coaches tour Vancouver, Victoria, and Whistler. They also offer double-deck bus tours to Vancouver attractions; the ticket is valid for two days. West Coast City & Nature Sightseeing provides mini-coach tours with a focus on natural sights. ✪ Gray Line of Vancouver: 604 879 3363 • Gray Line of Victoria: 250 388 5248 • West Coast City & Nature Sightseeing: 604 451 1600

5 First Nations Tours
Coast Salish guides lead two-hour interpretive paddles in a 12-passenger, traditional-style, ocean-going canoe. The protected waters of Burrard Inlet are the background for stories and songs that capture the rich culture of Northwest Coast First Nations. Kayaking is an alternative. All ages welcome, from May to October. ✪ Takaya Tours: 604 904 7410

6 Whale Watches
For sightings of orcas (killer whales), Dall's porpoises, seals, and other wildlife, Wild Whales Vancouver departs the harbor for the Gulf of Georgia and beyond. Vancouver Whale Watch has Zodiac-style boats with on-board naturalists. Steveston Seabreeze Adventures runs from the Fraser River to the Gulf Islands on larger vessels. ✪ Steveston Seabreeze Adventures: 604 272 7200 • Vancouver Whale Watch: 604 274 9565 • Wild Whales Vancouver: 604 699 2011

7 Horse-Drawn Tours
A century-old tradition, the Clydesdales-drawn narrated tours of Stanley Park run March to November. Up to 20 passengers per trolley. One-hour tours of Victoria visit Beacon Hill Park and other scenic spots. ✪ Stanley Park Tours: 604 681 5115 • www.stanleyparktours.com • Victoria Carriage Tours: 1 877 663 2207

8 Cycle Tours
Local guides oversee cycling, mountain biking, and multi-sport adventures. Gourmet meals, a stop at the hot springs, and luxurious support van included. Small groups. ✪ Rocky Mountain Cycle Tours: 604 898 8488 or 1 800 661 2453

9 Golf in Whistler
Let Eagle Tours plan your accommodation, transportation, and tee times at Whistler's five championship golf courses. All you have to do is play. ✪ Eagle Tours: 604 905 4035 or 1 888 793 9222

10 Rafting Trips
Whitewater rafting expeditions on the mighty Fraser, Thompson, and Nahatlatch rivers, from one to six days in length, are suited to various experience levels. Camp or enjoy B&B accommodations at the Yale base. ✪ Fraser River Raft Expeditions: 1 800 363 7238

Left **Telephone booth sign** Middle **Tickets Tonight sign** Right **Wheelchair access sign**

TOP 10 Useful Information

1 Media

The two largest newspapers in BC are produced in Vancouver, the *Vancouver Sun* and the *Vancouver Province*. The two national newspapers, the *Globe and Mail* and the *National Post*, are also available. Popular radio stations include CBC Radio Two (FM 105.7) for classical music, NEWS 1130 (AM 1130) for news, The FOX (FM 99.3) for rock music, and QMFM (FM103.5) for easy-listening music. The most popular Canadian TV stations are CBC, CTV, Global, Bravo, CityTV, and, in BC, the Knowledge Network.

2 Entertainment Listings

Georgia Straight, a weekly Vancouver tabloid, is available free at cafés, bars, bookshops, libraries, and street boxes. It is the best source to check the local music and art scene. For same-day savings on tickets to many events and performances, try Tickets Tonight at the Burrard St Tourist Infocentre *(see p108).* ✆ www.straight.com

3 Currency

The Canadian unit of currency is the dollar, which is divided into 100 cents. Coins come in denominations of 1, 5, 10, and 25 cents, and 1 and 2 dollars. Bank notes (bills) come in denominations of $5, $10, $20, $50, $100, and $500. Plan to

arrive with at least $100 in local currency and get change on arrival for tipping and transit.

4 Taxes

In Canada, taxes are not included in the listed price unless specified, so when making a purchase add a further 7 percent for PST (provincial sales tax) and 7 percent for GST (goods and services tax), except on alcohol, spirits and wines, which are taxed at 10 percent GST. An additional hotel room tax of between 8 and 10 percent is charged in BC. Some taxes are refundable when you leave Canada *(see p112).*

5 Websites

Helpful infomation for planning your trip to Vancouver, Victoria, and Whistler is available online. ✆ www.city.vancouver.bc.ca • www.tourismvancouver.bc.com • www.tourismvictoria.com • www.tourismwhistler.com

6 Telephones

Public telephones are often both coin- and card-operated. Local calls cost $0.25; directory assistance (411) is free. Most convenience stores sell phone cards. Within Greater Vancouver, you must prefix the local telephone number with area code 604. Long-distance calls in BC require either a 604 or 250 prefix. For a long-distance number in North America, dial the

prefix 1 and then the area code. To dial abroad, dial 011 + country code + city code (dropping the first 0)

7 Public Holidays

New Year's Day (Jan 1), Good Friday and Easter Monday (Mar or Apr), Victoria Day (usually 3rd Mon in May), Canada Day (Jul 1), BC Day (1st Mon in Aug), Labour Day (1st Mon in Sep), Thanksgiving (2nd Mon in Oct), Christmas Day (Dec 25), Boxing Day (Dec 26). Remembrance Day (Nov 11) is a holiday for banks and government offices.

8 Accessibility

Vancouver and Victoria work hard to make their attractions and services accessible but it is best to check ahead. In Vancouver, SeaBus and SkyTrain are accessible, and all SkyTrain stations have elevators. Lift and "kneeling" public transit buses for people with mobility aids operate on many routes in both cities *(see p107).*

9 Consulates

In emergencies, your consulate may be of assistance. ✆ UK: 800-1111 Melville St, 604 683 4421 • USA: 1095 W Pender St, 604 685 4311

10 Drinking

The legal drinking age in BC is 19. Consuming alcoholic beverages in public spaces is not allowed.

For more information about tax refunds for visitors to Canada, visit the website www.ccradrc.gc.ca/visitors

Left **Hospital sign** Middle **Police car** Right **No smoking zone**

10 Security & Health

1 Hotel Room Safety

When you've checked into your room, look on the back of the entrance door for a map showing the escape route to take in case of fire. Always leave the security latch in place when in your room and don't admit strangers. Some hotels have floors just for women – ask when booking, if you are a woman traveling alone.

2 Food Safety

City health officials inspect most Vancouver and Victoria food establishments, including pubs and delicatessens, regularly. Reports may be viewed online. ❂ www.foodinspectionweb.vcha.ca

3 Emergency Help

Various emergency and helplines are available to call in a crisis. ❂ Emergency and ambulance: 911 • Vancouver Police Department: 604 717 321 • Victoria Police Department: 250 995 7654 • BC Nurseline: 604 215 700 • VictimLINK: 1 800 63 0808

4 Public Transit

Skytrain platforms provide designated waiting areas in Vancouver; these are recommended at night. Available on most Victoria and Vancouver buses and some regional buses in BC, request Stop allows a woman to get off a bus at locations between

regular stops. Tell the driver at least one stop ahead of where you want to get off, and leave the bus by the front doors. The rear doors will remain closed so that no one can follow you off.

5 Know Your Surroundings

Carry a good map with you and check out the route to and from your destination before starting out. If you plan on returning late, make sure you have enough change and cash to call for and pay for a taxi. Avoid dark places such as parks and alleyways at night, especially if you are on your own, and avoid known danger spots (see p105).

6 Hospital Emergency Rooms

Emergency treatment is available 24 hours a day. ❂ Vancouver: Children's Hospital, 4500 Oak St, 604 875 2000; Lion's Gate Hospital, 231 E 15th St, 604 988 3131; St Paul's Hospital, 1081 Burrard St, 604 682 2344; Vancouver General, 899 West 12th Ave, 604 875 4111 • Victoria: Royal Jubilee Hospital, 1900 Fort St, 250 370 8000; Victoria General Hospital, 1 Hospital Way, 250 727 4212

7 Dental Emergencies

The BC Dental Association can link you with a nearby dentist during regular office hours.

After office hours, go to a hospital emergency room. ❂ British Columbia Dental Association • 604 736 7202

8 Smoking

Vancouver is a smoke-free city and smoking is not allowed in public spaces or workplaces. However, smoking is allowed on outdoor restaurant and bar patios.

9 Pharmacies

The majority of pharmacies in Vancouver and Victoria are open from 9am to 9 or 10pm. Some are open later. There are three 24-hour Shoppers Drug Mart pharmacies in Vancouver. The most central is on Davie Street. ❂ Vancouver: Shoppers Drug Mart, 1125 Davie St, 604 669 2424 • Victoria: London Drugs, 911 Yates St, 250 360 0880

10 Theft Prevention

To help prevent theft don't flash cash around. Your wallet or valuables should be stored close to your body, not in your backpack, back pocket, or belt-pack, where they can be easily pilfered. If you carry a purse, ensure it closes tightly. When leaving your hotel room – even just for a short time – first lock up valuables and important documents in your room's safe, if it has one. If it doesn't, have them put in the hotel's safe.

Left **Georgia Street rotunda, Pacific Centre** Right **Backpackers Shop**

Top 10 Shopping Tips

1 Store Hours
Most shops are open 10am to 6pm, Monday to Saturday (often later on Thursday). Department stores and shops in malls and retail districts may stay open to 9pm, Monday to Saturday, and open Sunday from 11am or noon to 5pm. Many shops close January 1, July 1, Labour Day, Thanksgiving and December 25.

2 Payment
MasterCard, American Express, and Visa credit cards are widely accepted, Diner's Club and Discovery less so. Debit cards compatible with Plus, Interac, or Cirrus systems are also widely accepted. You will need your PIN.

3 Sales & Returns
Excellent savings are to be had on Boxing Day (December 26). Sale items and sometimes those at full price may not be refundable, or exchangeable only. Be sure to ask about the return policy.

4 Department Stores
Vancouver's two department store chains, Sears and The Bay, carry practically everything. Holt Renfrew sells high-end clothing and accessories. The Bay also anchors Victoria's Bay Centre. ◊ *Holt Renfrew: Pacific Centre, 633 Granville St • Map K3 • Sears: Pacific Centre, 701 Granville St • Map K3 • The Bay: 647 Granville St,* *Vancouver • Map K3 • The Bay: 1150 Douglas St, Victoria • Map P2*

5 Shopping Malls
The largest downtown mall is Pacific Centre *(see p55)*. Other malls include Sinclair Centre *(see p54)*, and Metrotown *(see p55)*. Victoria's Bay Centre has over 80 shops. Market Square's shops are in heritage buildings. ◊ *Bay Centre: 1150 Douglas St • Map P2 • Market Square: 560 Johnson St • Map P2*

6 Music
A&B Sound may have the lowest prices in town. Classical and jazz lovers should head to the Magic Flute. For vinyl, try Neptoon Records. Lyle's Place in Victoria sells new and used CDs, from jazz to punk rock. ◊ *A&B Sound: 556 Seymour St • Map K3 • Magic Flute: 2203 W 4th Ave • Map B2 • Neptoon Records: 3561 Main St • Map B2 • Lyle's Place: 770 Yates St • Map Q2*

7 Books
Chapters and Book Warehouse have good selections and several locations. Used-book seller MacLeod's specializes in Canadiana and history. Visit Duthie Books for contemporary literature, and Kidsbooks for children's titles. Munro's of Victoria sells a range of titles. ◊ *Book Warehouse: 550 Granville St • Map K3 • Chapters: 788 Robson St • Map K4 • Duthie Books:* *2239 W 4th Ave • Map B2 • Kidsbooks: 3083 W Broadway • Map A2 • MacLeod's: 455 W Pender St • Map L... • Munro's: 1108 Government St • Map P2*

8 Alcohol
Alcohol sales are restricted to BC government Liquor Stores (wine, spirits, and beer), private wine sellers, Vintners Quality Assurance (VQA) outlets (specializing in B... wines), and Cold Beer Stores. ◊ *Liquor Store: 1120 Alberni St • Map J3 • Village VQA Wines: 3536 W 41st Ave • Map A2 • Wine Barrel: 644 Broughton St, Victoria • Map P3*

9 Convenience Stores
Small shops selling cigarettes, toiletries, cold drinks, snacks, and lotter... tickets are ubiquitous in Vancouver and Victoria. Some also sell public transit tickets.

10 Tax Refunds
Books and groceries are exempt from the 7 percent provincial sales tax; most other items are subject to up to 14 percent sales tax *(see p110)*. International visitors who spent over $200 may be entitled to a refund of the 7 percen... GST (goods and service... tax), excluding GST on restaurant meals, drinks, tobacco, and transport. Save the receipts. ◊ *Visitor Rebate Program 1 800 668 4748*

BC specialities include Okanagan wines, ice wine, smoked salmon, and First Nations art and jewelry

Left **Bedroom, Pacific Palisades Hotel** Left **Wines, Don Francesco restaurant**

Accommodation & Dining Tips

1 Hotel Taxes
In BC, accommodation is taxed with an 8 percent accommodation tax and a 7 percent GST (goods and services tax). An additional 2 percent tourism tax is levied on hotel rooms in Vancouver, Victoria, and Whistler. You may be entitled to a GST refund for short hotel stays.

2 Rooms
Most hotel rooms are well furnished and of a good size. Most have two double beds or one queen- or king-sized bed; twin-bedded rooms may also be available. If you are sensitive to noise, ask for a room away from the elevator and the ice and dispensing machines. About 85 percent of rooms in Vancouver, Victoria, and Whistler are smoke-free.

3 Rack Rates
Hotel rates vary according to the hotel category, the day of week, and season. Peak rates are weekdays and from April to December. Rack rates, the basic room rates, are the ones used in this book to provide a guide price. It is usually possible to get a better deal, especially if booking online. Discounts are often available to students, members of clubs such as auto associations, or the Elderhostel. When booking, ask what special rates apply and bring proof of membership with you.

4 Concierges
Mid- and large-size hotels have concierges on staff whose job it is to cater to the needs and whims of the guests. They will procure tickets to shows and sports games, make restaurant reservations, arrange transportation, and offer helpful tips.

5 Extra Costs
Parking at downtown hotels can be costly, so inquire about rates (taxes also apply). Some hotels do offer free parking. Telephone calls made from your room phone can be pricey, as are drinks and snacks consumed from the room's minibar. These costs can add up quickly, and will appear on your final room bill.

6 Restaurant Reservations
Most restaurants take reservations. It's a good idea to book a table at a popular dining spot on arriving or even in advance of your trip. Mention if you have special needs or dietary requirements. It is considered good form to cancel your reservation if your plans change.

7 Tipping
Tips and service charges are not usually added to dining bills, though they may be if your party consists of six people or more. For service at restaurants, cafés, and clubs, plan on tipping about 15 percent of the pre-tax amount. An easy way of estimating the tip is to add up the taxes on the bill. At bars, leave a dollar or two for the bartender. Tip porters and bellhops at least $1 per bag or suitcase; cloakroom attendants $1 per garment and chambermaids, a minimum of $1 to $2 per day. A hotel doorman will also appreciate a dollar or two for his services.

8 Dress Codes
Jacket and tie are almost never required in restaurants, though many diners opt to wear them on a special evening out, especially to an upscale place. Some clubs, however, may not allow you in if you are wearing sneakers or jeans.

9 Cell Phones
At most restaurants, it is considered discourteous to leave your cell phone turned on or to carry on cell phone conversations.

10 Meal Times
Breakfast is usually served in diners and coffee shops from about 6am to 10am. Lunch is available from about 11:30am to 2pm, dinner from about 5pm to 10pm. Many pubs and restaurants offer a late-night menu. Brunches are often served on weekends only – and at some spots, on Sundays only – usually from 11am to 2pm or later.

Accommodation rates are often lower in winter months, except for the weeks around Christmas and New Year's

Left **Sylvia Hotel** Right **Lobby, Inn at False Creek**

TOP 10 Inexpensive Hotels

1 Sylvia Hotel, Vancouver

The West End's grande dame is a favorite, not only for its relaxed yet sophisticated atmosphere, but also for its fabulous location right on English Bay. Some rooms are tiny, but the big draws are the lounge and restaurant overlooking the water. Covered paid parking available. ◎ *1154 Gilford St • Map G2 • 604 681 9321 • www. sylviahotel.com • $$*

2 Oceanside Hotel, Vancouver

Located on a quiet side street near English Bay and Stanley Park, this hotel is a friendly oasis in the heart of the West End. One-bedroom apartments and larger available. Free parking. ◎ *1847 Pendrell St • Map G2 • 604 682 5641 • www.oceanside-hotel.com • $$*

3 Inn at False Creek, Vancouver

Decorated Santa Fe-style, this modern, spotless hotel offers large, well-appointed rooms and executive suites. A knock-out location, steps from downtown and Granville Island. ◎ *1335 Howe St • Map J4 • 604 682 0229 • www.qualityhotel.ca • $$*

4 Sandman Suites on Davie, Vancouver

Recent extensive renovations make this West End high-rise a find. One-bedroom suites offer kitchens, washer/dryers, balconies, and sofa beds in the living room. The views of English Bay from many of the rooms are a plus. Underground paid parking available. ◎ *1160 Davie St • Map H4 • 604 681 7263 • www.sandman hotels.com • $$*

5 Bosman's Hotel, Vancouver

This hotel's draws include its convenient, central location, air-conditioned comfort, heated outdoor pool, and free parking. A restaurant and cozy lounge are also found onsite. Family owned for over 25 years. ◎ *1060 Howe St • Map J4 • 604 682 3171 • www.bosmanshotel.com • $$*

6 Greenbrier Hotel, Vancouver

Providing a great Robson Street location, this modest hotel's renovated one-bedroom suites have complete kitchens, with other pluses such as free coffee and free parking thrown in. ◎ *1393 Robson St • Map J3 • 604 683 4558 • www.greenbrier hotel.com • $$*

7 Buchan Hotel, Vancouver

This 1926-vintage, three-story property offers good value for money with its European-style, no-frills accommodation and its location: you'd be hard-pressed to sleep closer to Stanley Park – unless you were actually in it.

◎ *1906 Haro St • Map H2 • 604 685 5354 • www. buchanhotel.com • $$*

8 Best Western Chateau Granville, Vancouver

A frequent choice for out-of-towners with an eye for price and location, this 15-story hotel offers mainly one-bedroom suites, but has some smaller, standard rooms as well. Suites come with microwaves and wireless internet access. Gated parking available for a fee. ◎ *1100 Granville St • Map J4 • 604 669 7070 • www.bwcg.com • $$*

9 Traveller's Inn, Victoria

Voted Victoria's best value hotel/motel five years running (1999–2003), this downtown property scores with its air-conditioned rooms – most with king-sized beds and some with kitchens – and free parking. Passes to local pools also provided. ◎ *710 Queens Ave • 250 380 1000 • www. travellersinn.com • $$*

10 Admiral Inn, Victoria

Popular with families, seniors, and those in search of a room with an Inner Harbour view at a reasonable price, this family-run property provides its guests with spotless rooms, free bike rental, and free parking, among other niceties. ◎ *257 Belleville St • Map N4 • 250 388 1000 • www.admiral.bc.ca • $$*

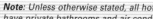
***Note:** Unless otherwise stated, all hotels accept credit cards and have private bathrooms and air conditioning*

Price Categories

For a standard, double room per night (with breakfast if included), taxes and extra charges.		
$	under $100
$$	$100–150
$$$	$150–200
$$$$	$200–300
$$$$$	over $300

Above **Granville Island Hotel**

🏨10 Mid-Priced Hotels

1 Days Inn Vancouver Downtown

Although the heritage building housing this small hotel was built in 1910, the simple but comfortable rooms have been fully renovated. A restaurant and lounge are found onsite, while myriad dining and sightseeing options are within walking distance. 🆂 *921 W Pender St • Map K3 • 604 681 4335 • www.daysinnvancouver. com • $$$*

2 Granville Island Hotel, Vancouver

With delightful rooms overlooking False Creek, this intimate hotel, located right on Granville Island, features wooden shutters, beamed ceilings, and oversized bath tubs. Dine at the Dockside restaurant, or choose from the many nearby eateries. 🆂 *1253 Johnston St • Map H5 • 604 683 7373 • www.granvilleisland hotel.com • $$$*

3 Georgian Court Hotel, Vancouver

Providing a great location for sports fans in town to take in a game – BC Place Stadium and GM Place are mere minutes away – this well-appointed hotel offers air-conditioned rooms, fitness center, and complimentary internet. Enjoy the two on-site restaurants, including the renowned William Tell. 🆂 *773 Beatty St • Map K4 • 604 682 5555 • www.georgian court.com • $$$*

4 Crowne Plaza Hotel Georgia, Vancouver

This downtown heritage hotel has undergone significant upgrades, including the addition of custom-designed furniture and Canadian art. Facilities include two restaurants and a fitness center. 🆂 *801 W Georgia St • Map K3 • 604 682 5566 • www.hotelgeorgia. bc.ca • $$$*

5 Ramada Inn and Suites Downtown, Vancouver

Art Deco touches enhance this downtown hotel. A great spot if you want to be as close to clubs and shops as to most central attractions. Air-conditioned rooms; pets welcomed for a fee. 🆂 *1221 Granville St • Map J4 • 604 685 1111 • www.ramada vancouver.com • $$*

6 Blue Horizon Hotel, Vancouver

Gorgeous views abound, as each room in this contemporary hotel has wraparound windows and balcony. Add to that the duvets, fridges, coffee makers, air conditioning, and more. 🆂 *1225 Robson St • Map J3 • 604 688 1411 • www.blue horizonhotel.com • $$$*

7 Century Plaza Hotel & Spa, Vancouver

Renovated in 2003, the hotel is a modest, good-value choice. The big draw here is the European-style spa *(see p56)* with indoor pool and steam room. The lounge, restaurant, and cappuccino bar are handy, too. 🆂 *1015 Burrard St • Map J4 • 604 687 0575 • www.century-plaza.com • $$$*

8 Bedford Regency Hotel, Victoria

Old World charm is enhanced by the views of Victoria's harbor. Try the in-room Jacuzzi, then snuggle in a goose down comforter. Rooms are air-conditioned, with free internet access and coffee. 🆂 *1140 Government St • Map P2 • 250 384 6835 • www.bedfordregency .com • $$$*

9 Gatsby Mansion Inn, Victoria

Period furniture sets the mood in this heritage Victorian mansion on the Inner Harbour. An on-site restaurant and garden add to the gracious ambience. 🆂 *309 Belleville St • Map N4 • 250 388 9191 • www.bellevillepark.com • $$$*

10 Quality Inn Downtown, Victoria

This pleasant spot, only two blocks from Victoria's Inner Harbour, offers fairly large rooms with kitchenettes. Free in-room tea, coffee and local calls, plus an indoor pool, and steam and fitness rooms. 🆂 *850 Blanshard St • Map Q3 • 250 385 6787 • www.victoriaquality inn.com • $$$*

Left **Lobby, Fairmont Hotel Vancouver** Right **Bedroom, Opus Hotel Vancouver**

10 Luxury & Boutique Hotels

1 Opus Hotel Vancouver
Opened in 2002, this stylish boutique hotel is a Yaletown trendsetter. Take advantage of the on-site French brasserie and sophisticated lounge to relax after a busy day. ⊗ 322 Davie St • Map J5 • 604 642 6787 • www. opushotel.com • $$$$

2 Pacific Palisades, Vancouver
You may catch a glimpse of a Hollywood star at this stylish South Beach-inspired hotel. The decor is fun yet functional, with full guest services and amenities. Step outside to Robson Street and join the passing parade. ⊗ 1277 Robson St • Map J3 • 604 688 0461 • www.pacificpalisades hotel.com • $$$$

3 Listel Vancouver Hotel
A beautiful boutique hotel whose rooms are filled with art by top local artists and supplied with literary gems, some by West Coast authors. O'Doul's Restaurant and Bar (see p74) provides nightly live music. ⊗ 1300 Robson St • Map J3 • 604 684 8461 • www.listel-vancouver. com • $$$$

4 Hotel Le Soleil, Vancouver
A chic downtown boutique hotel with nice touches, such as a turn-down service, cordless phones, bathrobes,

concierge, valet parking, and room service. Pets are welcome for a fee. ⊗ 567 Hornby St • Map K3 • 604 632 3000 • www. lesoleilhotel.com • $$$$

5 Wedgewood Hotel, Vancouver
Owner Eleni Skalbania is as famous as her boutique hotel with its European flair. Caters to those who prefer their accommodation upscale, verging on exclusive. Maid service twice daily says it all. ⊗ 845 Hornby St • Map J3 • 604 689 7777 • www.wedgewoodhotel. com • $$$$

6 Fairmont Hotel Vancouver
Vancouver grew up with this classic hotel, which opened in 1939. Renovated several times, it includes an indoor pool, day spa, and health club to erase the day's exertions. Enjoy refreshments in the deluxe lobby lounge, reminiscent of the grand old days. ⊗ 900 W Georgia St • Map J3 • 604 684 3131 • www.fairmont.com/ hotelvancouver • $$$$$

7 Metropolitan Hotel, Vancouver
Everything is done to cosset guests, including European down duvets, marble bathrooms, indoor pool and health club, business center, restaurant, and lounge. An award-winning gem. One smoking floor. ⊗ 645 Howe St • Map K3

• 604 687 1122 • www.metropolitan.com • $$$$

8 Fairmont Empress Hotel, Victoria
The most famous hotel on the West Coast, Victoria's luxury property offers somewhat small but always elegant rooms. Make a reservation to take English-style tea in its glorious lobby (see p99), a pricey but noteworthy experience. ⊗ 721 Government St • Map P4 • 250 384 8111 • www. fairmont.com/ empress • $$$$$

9 Wickaninnish Inn, Long Beach
Perched dramatically on a rocky shelf overlooking Chesterman Beach, this highly acclaimed inn offers luxurious lodgings done in modern West Coast style. With its gorgeous spa and gourmet restaurant, this is the perfect getaway spot (see pp32–3). ⊗ Osprey Lane, Tofino • Map A4 • 250 725 3100 • www.wick inn.com • $$$$$

10 Sooke Harbour House, Sooke
Beauty is the hallmark of this lovely inn 19 miles (30 km) west of Victoria. Rooms are filled with antiques and coastal-themed art. Add the ocean views, luxury spa services, and an organic garden providing produce for its world-renowned cuisine. ⊗ 1528 Whiffen Spit Rd • Map D6 • 250 642 3421 • www.sookeharbour house.com • $$$$$

Note: Unless otherwise stated, all hotels accept credit cards and have private bathrooms and air conditioning

Price Categories

For a standard, double room per night (with breakfast if included), taxes and extra charges.

$	under $100
$$	$100–150
$$$	$150–200
$$$$	$200–300
$$$$$	over $300

Above **Pan Pacific Vancouver**

🔟 Business & Suite Hotels

1 Pan Pacific Vancouver

Soaring over the waterfront, the Pan's rooms and luxury suites provide spectacular views of the North Shore mountains. The convention center is in the same complex. Regarded as North America's premiere convention hotel. ◊ 300-999 Canada Place • Map L2 • 604 662 8111 • http://vancouver.pan pacific.com • $$$$$

2 Coast Plaza Hotel and Suites, Vancouver

Located in the West End, this award-winning hotel offers rooms and suites, 22 meeting rooms, a garden terrace, restaurant, 24-hour room service, and a well-appointed health club. ◊ 1763 Comox St • Map G2 • 604 688 7711 • www.coasthotels.com • $$$$

3 Delta Vancouver Suite Hotel

An all-suite luxury hotel, centrally located, offering state-of-the-art in-room technology, comfort, and convenience. A restaurant, lounge, and full health club round out the amenities. ◊ 550 W Hastings St • Map K3 • 604 689 8188 • www.deltahotels.com • $$$$

4 Fairmont Waterfront, Vancouver

Linked to the convention center by an enclosed walkway, this harborside property has been voted the top hotel in Canada by Condé Nast magazine readers. Amenities include Fairmont Gold concierge service, and a year-round outdoor heated pool. Rooms are plush, tranquil. ◊ 900 Canada Place Way • Map L3 • 604 691 1991 • www.fairmont.com/ waterfront • $$$$$

5 Four Seasons Hotel, Vancouver

The ideal business location, centrally located above the Pacific Centre Mall, this hotel goes the extra mile, with a 24-hour concierge, health club, indoor/outdoor pool, catering, meeting facilities, 24-hour room service, and valet parking. ◊ 791 W Georgia St • Map K3 • 604 689 9333 • www.fourseasons.com/ vancouver • $$$$$

6 Lord Stanley Suites on the Park, Vancouver

Furnished one- and two-bedroom suites close to Stanley Park are a good choice for extended stays. Free continental breakfast, underground parking, fitness center, and sauna. ◊ 1889 Alberni St • Map H2 • 604 688 9299 • www.lordstanley.com • $$$$

7 Meridian at 910 Beach, Vancouver

Offers a variety of fully equipped suites, some with goodies such as in-suite washer and dryer. Rates include continental breakfast and use of the fitness center. Underground paid parking. ◊ 910 Beach Ave • Map H5 • 604 609 5100 • www.meridianhotel.org • $$$

8 Sunset Inn and Suites, Vancouver

Found in the lively West End in a high-rise building, this property's location is nonetheless off the main thoroughfare, so quieter than some. Suitable for short- and long-term stays; rooms come with free high-speed, wireless internet. ◊ 1111 Burnaby St • Map H4 • 604 688 2474 • www.sunsetinn.com • $$$

9 Laurel Point Inn, Victoria

Spacious rooms come with a view of Victoria's Inner Harbour. The Sunday buffet-style brunch in the Terrace Room is a must. ◊ 680 Montreal St • 250 386 8721 • www.laurelpoint.com • $$$$

10 Swans Suite Hotel, Victoria

An award-winning heritage hotel in the heart of Victoria's Old Town. Enjoy its extensive art collection, plus suites with kitchens, loft bedrooms, and feather duvets. On-site brewpub, bistro, and wine-and-beer shop. The rooftop penthouse offers panoramic views. ◊ 506 Pandora Ave • Map P1 • 250 361 3310 • www. swanshotel.com • $$$

Streetsmart

Left **Guestroom, O Canada House** Right **Front porch, West End Guest House**

Bed & Breakfasts

1 O Canada House, Vancouver

Built in 1897, this delightful guesthouse reflects the early elegance of the West End, including a parlor with a fireplace. King- and queen-bedded rooms with private baths. Gourmet breakfast included.
⊗ 1114 Barclay St
• Map J3 • 604 688 0555
• www.ocanadahouse.com
• $$$$

2 West End Guest House, Vancouver

A pretty pink and white 1906 Victorian inn near Stanley Park offering one- and two-bedroom suites. Free parking, bike storage, telephones in rooms. Full hot breakfast served.
⊗ 1362 Haro St • Map J3
• 604 681 2889
• www.westendguest house.com • $$$

3 Corkscrew Inn B&B, Vancouver

In a lovely restored 1912 Craftsman-style house, this funky Kitsilano B&B combines Art Deco charm – including dozens of stained-glass windows – with upscale amenities, such as feather beds, robes, and high-speed internet. Take a peek at the curios in the small wine museum.
⊗ 2735 W 2nd Ave • Map B2 • 604 733 7276 • www. corkscrewinn.com • $$$

4 English Bay Inn, Vancouver

A West End hideaway with cozy antique furniture, queen-sized beds, and ensuite bathrooms. The full breakfast by the fireplace is a pleasant start to the day. Free parking.
⊗ 1968 Comox St • Map G2 • 604 683 8002 • www. englishbayinn.com • $$$$

5 Jolly Taxpayer B&B Hotel & Pub, Vancouver

Located near Gastown and the waterfront, the 28 European-style units are set in a quaint, restored heritage building, which also houses a pub. Free continental breakfast.
⊗ 828 W Hastings St
• Map K3 • 604 681 3550
• www.jollytaxpayerhotel. com • $$

6 Victorian Hotel, Vancouver

Built in 1898 as one of the city's first guesthouses, this hotel has been carefully restored to retain its Victorian-era ambience, with bay windows, high ceilings, antique furnishings, and hardwood floors. A comfortable setting, with beautiful bathrooms and down duvets on the beds. Secured parking available for a fee.
⊗ 514 Homer St • Map L3
• 604 681 6369 • www. victorianhotel.ca • $$

7 Barclay House B&B, Vancouver

A perennial West End favorite, this classic 1904 home features spacious two-room suites, attentive staff, a full three-course breakfast, afternoon sherry, in-room portable phones, and more. Free parking.
⊗ 1351 Barclay St • Map H3 • 604 605 1351 • www barclayhouse.com • $$$

8 Abigail's Hotel, Victoria

A heritage, Tudor-style B&B-inn with English-style gardens. Charming touches, such as country furnishings, fresh flowers, and a gourmet breakfast. Some rooms with whirlpool tubs or wood-burning fireplaces. ⊗ 906 McClure St • 250 388 5363 • www.abigails hotel.com • $$$$$

9 Heathergate House, Victoria

A near-perfect location on Victoria's busy Inner Harbour, yet a quiet environment. The invitingly posh rooms all have private bath. A well-appointed garden cottage easily sleeps four. Full English breakfast included.
⊗ 122 Simcoe St
• 250 383 0068
• www.heathergatebb. com • $$

10 Beaconsfield Inn, Victoria

Dark mahogany floors, antiques, fireplaces, featherbeds, and private bathrooms all add to the stately ambience at this award-winning 1905 Victoria heritage manor. Full breakfast, English tea, and daily sherry included.
⊗ 998 Humboldt St
• 250 384 4044
• www.beaconsfieldinn. com • $$$

For more bed & breakfasts, visit the website www.bedandbreakfasts-bc.com

Above **Entrance, YWCA Hotel/Residence**

Price Categories

For a standard, double room per night (with breakfast if included), taxes and extra charges.	
$	under $100
$$	$100–150
$$$	$150–200
$$$$	$200–300
$$$$$	over $300

10 Budget Accommodation

1 University of British Columbia, Vancouver

From May to August, take your pick of 3,000 rooms on UBC's beautiful campus. Year-round, one-bedroom suites with kitchens are available. UBC is a city in itself, with many amenities on its grounds. ✆ 5961 Student Union Blvd • Map A2 • 604 822 1000 • www.ubcconferences.com • $

2 YWCA Hotel/Residence, Vancouver

A secure, 12-story high-rise with air-conditioned rooms to suit all travelers, including families. A good location for those who need their gym fix, with free admission to the fitness center. TVs in some rooms. Wheelchair accessible. ✆ 733 Beatty St • Map L4 • 604 895 5830 • www.ywcahotel.com • $

3 Hostelling International Vancouver Downtown

Shared and private rooms are offered in this friendly West End spot. Free breakfast is served, while the shared kitchen can help with the other meals. Internet access and secure storage lockers. Open 24 hours. ✆ 1114 Burnaby St • Map H4 • 604 684 4565 • www.hihostels.ca • $

4 Hostelling International Vancouver Central

The newest HI Vancouver hostel, with private rooms as well as traditional dormitory rooms. Efficiently run, and located in the heart of Vancouver's nightclub district. A laundry, kitchen, and bar all onsite. ✆ 1025 Granville St • Map J4 • 604 685 5335 • www.hihostels.ca • $

5 Hostelling International Vancouver Jericho Beach

This hostel is a 30-minute bus ride from downtown and worth the trip. Open 24 hours, this beachside spot features shared and private rooms and a cook-it-yourself, shared kitchen. Secure storage lockers. Closed during the winter season. ✆ 1515 Discovery St • Map A2 • 604 224 3208 • www.hihostels.ca/vancouverjerichobeach • $

6 Dominion Hotel, Vancouver

Ideal for adventurous travelers, this renovated Gastown hotel at Abbott and Water streets dates back to 1899. But turn-of-the-19th-century architecture is presented with a new twist: art-concept rooms designed by local artists. ✆ 210 Abbott St • Map L3 • 604 681 6666 • www.dominionhotel.ca • $

7 Kingston Hotel, Vancouver

A relaxed, spotless 1910 heritage building with private and shared baths, a TV lounge, day and overnight storage, sauna, and restaurant. Free continental breakfast. ✆ 757 Richards St • Map K4 • 604 684 9024 • www.kingstonhotelvancouver.com • $

8 C & N Backpackers Hostel, Victoria

Just-off-central location with transit and bus depot nearby. Renovated with new beds, bathrooms, shared kitchens, and internet. Clean, private and shared non-smoking rooms, with single-sex dorms. Some rooms with TV. ✆ 927 Main St • 604 682 2441 • www.cnnbackpackers.com • $

9 Ocean Island Backpackers Inn, Victoria

Clean, comfortable and funky, the site is a secure historic building near Victoria's Inner Harbour. Dorms and private rooms with 24-hour check-in. ✆ 791 Pandora St • Map Q2 • 250 385 1788/9 • www.oceanisland.com • $

10 Hotel Douglas, Victoria

This downtown Victoria character hotel exudes 19th-century charm. The lounge attracts a friendly, well-dressed mix, with live music on weekends, including jazz nights. Wheelchair accessibility. Free parking. ✆ 1450 Douglas St • Map Q2 • 250 383 4157 • www.hoteldouglas.com • $

Some accomodations, especially those in private homes or heritage buildings, are not wheelchair accessible. Check before booking.

General Index

Acknowledgments

The Author
Long time BC resident Constance Brissenden lives in downtown Vancouver. She has written numerous travel, history, and children's books, and is co-author of the Dorling Kindersley *Eyewitness Travel Guide to the Pacific Northwest*.

Produced by International Book Productions Inc., Toronto

Editorial Director
Barbara Hopkinson
Art Editor James David Ellis
Editors Judy Phillips, Sheila Hall
Senior DTP Designer
Dietmar Kokemohr
Photo Research and Permissions
Sheila Hall
Proofreader Helen Townsend
Indexer Barbara Sale Schon

Photographer
Cylla von Tiedemann

AT DORLING KINDERSLEY
Senior Editor Kathryn Lane
Art Editor Shahid Mahmood
Publishing Manager Jane Ewart
Publisher Douglas Amrine
Senior Cartographic Editor
Casper Morris
Senior DTP Designer Jason Little
Production Louise Daly
Maps Mapping Ideas Ltd.
DK Picture Library
Romaine Werblow

Picture Credits
t-top; tl-top left; tlc-top left centre; tc-top centre; tr-top right; cla-centre left above; ca-centre above; cra-centre right above; cl-centre left; c-centre; cr-centre right; clb-centre left below; cb-centre below; crb-centre right below; bl-bottom left, b-bottom; bc-bottom centre; bcl-bottom centre left; br-bottom right; sb-sidebar.

Every effort has been made to trace the copyright holders, and we apologize for any unintentional omissions. We would be pleased to insert the appropriate acknowledgments in any subsequent edition of this publication.

The publishers would like to thank the following individuals, companies, and picture libraries for their kind permission to reproduce their photographs:

ALCAN DRAGON BOAT FESTIVAL: Jessica Bushey 44c

BARD ON THE BEACH SHAKESPEARE FESTIVAL staging of Much Ado About Nothing (2004): 44tl
BC PLACE: 42tr
BLUE WATER CAFE: 40br
BUTCHART GARDENS LTD, Victoria, BC Canada: 38tl, 101tr

CANADA PLACE CORPORATION: 4–5
CAPILANO SUSPENSION BRIDGE: 6clb, 14crb, 14–15c, 15tc, 15bl, 46br, 84cr
CITY OF VANCOUVER ARCHIVES: 11cr, 31cra
CITY OF VANCOUVER: *Inukshuk* by Alvin Kanak 1986 8tl, *The Crab* by George Norris 1968 34br, *Captain John Deighton (Gassy Jack)* by Vern Simpson 1970 60cra, *Gate to the Northwest Passage* by Alan Chung Hung 1980 76tl
CN IMAX THEATRE: 13bc
CYPRESS MOUNTAIN: 48tr

FAIRMONT HOTELS & RESORTS: 30tl, 64tr, 69tr, 92–3, 116tl
FOUR SEASONS RESORT WHISTLER: Michael Rafelson 29tl, 57tl

GRANVILLE ISLAND MUSEUMS: 21bc, 35tr
GROUSE MOUNTAIN RESORT: 3tr

HARBOUR CENTRE/THE LOOKOUT!:
51b, 66–7
HSBC CELEBRATION OF LIGHT: 44bl

INN AT FALSE CREEK: 114tr

METROPOLITAN HOTELS: 41t
MUSEUM OF ANTHROPOLOGY AT
UBC: *The Raven and the First Men* by
Bill Reid 1980 34ca, 36tl

NEW-SMALL & STERLING, LTD: 54cb

OPUS HOTEL: 116tr

PACIFIC PALISADES HOTEL: 113tl
PRINCE OF WHALES WHALE WATCH-
ING: 100tl

ROYAL BRITISH COLUMBIA MUSEUM:
7cla, 24cb, 24cla, 25tl, 25cr, 96tr

SCIENCE WORLD BC: 23tl
SQUAMISH CHAMBER OF COM-
MERCE/www.squamish.ca: Garry
Broeckling 87cl; Todd Lawson 49sb,
89tl; Bill McComish 39sb, 89tr
STORYEUM: 6bl, 16–17 all

TOURISM VANCOUVER ISLAND: 26–7c

VANCOUVER AQUARIUM: 10tr, 10tl,
10c, 11bl, 46tr
VANCOUVER ART GALLERY: Emily Carr,
Logger's Culls, 1935, oil on canvas,
Collection of the Vancouver Art Gallery,
Gift of Miss I. Parkyn, VAG 39.1, Photo:

Trevor Mills 18–19c; Robert Davidson,
Eagles, 1991, gouache and watercolour
on paper, Vancouver Art Gallery Acquisi-
tion Fund, VAG 94.3, Photo: Teresa Healy
19bl; Ken Lum, *Four Boats Stranded:
Red and Yellow, Black and White*, 2000,
polyurethane, steel, fiberglass, and
paint, Vancouver Art Gallery Major Pur-
chase Fund, the Canada Millennium
Bureau and the BC 2000 Community
Spirit Fund; VAG 2000.25 a-d, Photo:
Colin Goldie 18bc; 18cla
VANCOUVER CIVIC THEATRES: 42tl, 43tr
VANCOUVER MUSEUM, CANADA
(QFA 233): 76tr
VANCOUVER SYMPHONY ORCHES-
TRA: 45sb
VIDA WELLNESS SPAS: 56tl

WEDGEWOOD HOTEL: 40tr
WHISTLER BLACKCOMB RESORT:
Therese Lundgren 3br, Insight Photogra-
phy 7crb, Toshi Kawano 28–9c, 30tr
WICKANINNISH INN: 32–3

YVR ART FEDERATION: *The Spirit of
Haida Gwaii: The Jade Canoe* by Bill
Reid 1994, Photo: Bill MacLennan 34c;
Coast Salish Welcome Figures by Susan
Point 1996, Photo: Kenji Nagai 37bl

All other images are © Dorling
Kindersley. For further information see
www.dkimages.com

Special Editions of DK Travel Guides

DK Travel Guides can be purchased
in bulk quantities at discounted prices
for use in promotions or as premiums.
We are also able to offer special edi-
tions and personalized jackets, corpo-
rate imprints, and excerpts from all of
our books, tailored specifically to meet
your own needs.

To find out more, please contact:

(in the United States)
SpecialSales@dk.com

(in the UK) **Sarah.Burgess@dk.com**

(in Canada) DK Special Sales at
general@tourmaline.ca

(in Australia) **business.development
@pearson.com.au**

Selected Street Index